# PERTWEE'S
## PROMENADES
### and
## PIERROTS

One Hundred Years of
Seaside Entertainment

# PERTWEE'S
## PROMENADES
### and
## PIERROTS

### One Hundred Years of
### Seaside Entertainment

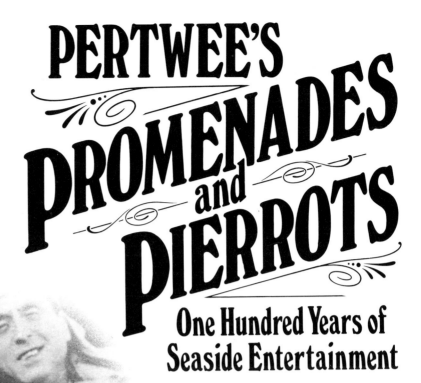

WESTBRIDGE BOOKS
A Division of David & Charles

Pierrots on the beach at Scarborough. Many
indoor pitches would have been proud of an
audience that size

**British Library Cataloguing in Publication Data**

Pertwee, Bill
    Pertwee's promenades and pierrots.
    1.   Vaudeville – Great Britain – History
    2.   Seaside resorts – Great Britain – History
    I.   Promenades and pierrots
    792.7         PN1968.G7

    ISBN 0–7153–7794–9

© Bill Pertwee 1979

Typeset by Trade Linotype Ltd
and printed in Great Britain
by Morrison and Gibb Ltd, Edinburgh
for Westbridge Books
(A Division of David & Charles)
Brunel House Newton Abbot Devon

Published in the United States of America
by David & Charles Inc
North Pomfret Vermont 05053 USA

Watching the pierrots at Holey Rock, Roker,
Sunderland, about 1910

In the middle of the nineteenth century the coming of the railways opened up many resorts to people who, until then, had only heard of them and imagined them as a sort of Shangri-La.

If you were lucky enough to be working—either as housemaid, cook or nannie to the fairly well-off middle class, or very well-off upper class (our language has never really found a substitute for the word 'class')—then you would probably accompany your master and mistress and family to whatever resort they favoured. Normally, the same one each year. This habit-forming routine was to be carried on well into the twentieth century and was mainly responsible for the success of seaside shows as an established form of entertainment.

If the family or families you were part of, or worked for, were not quite well-off enough to stay at a hotel for the summer at the resort of their choice, then they would take a house and life would carry on much as it did at home. Not just for a week or two—as now—but for four or five months. The menfolk would join their wives for most weekends and return to their businesses each Monday. The children, if they were old enough, would be away at boarding school and would join their families for the school summer holidays. This meant that for a fair amount of time 'mother' would have time on her hands and the servants would have more free time than they were normally used to. A walk on the 'prom' then became a fairly regular occurrence and quite an exciting event; after all, what could be nicer than a breath of sea air, a visit to the bandstand and perhaps—whatever your social position—a slight flirtation with the

Victoria Pier, Blackpool.

On the Palace Pier,                              Brighton.

West Pier, Brighton

opposite sex, which there was rarely time for during the winter months in London or any other of the great cities?

The earliest entertainments on the beach were the Punch and Judy shows, ice cream vendors, ginger beer men, quack doctors, palmists, wrestlers, musicians, and a variety of vendors selling newspapers, magazines, balloons, windmills, monkey nuts and sweets. A little later the 'sand artists' appeared, creating beautiful pictures in the sand. The tide would wash away their efforts each day but, undaunted, they would begin again the following day (actor John le Mesurier portrayed a sand artist in Tony Hancock's *The Punch and Judy Man* in the 1950s). Religious fanatics and soap-box orators, taking advantage of a ready-made crowd, would inform passers by how wicked they were to be even strolling about breathing the sea air.

By this time, most resorts had built or were building piers. A walk on the pier was, to some, the nearest they would ever get to the atmosphere of 'going across the water'. Some of these piers were modest, others—as at Blackpool, Brighton and the larger resorts—had concert halls, liberally decorated with palms and ferns, where one could listen in the afternoon to small orchestras— violinists hell-bent on ruining the hearing of anyone within fifty feet of them; bass players permanently stuck round their instruments, making them easily recognisable away from their jobs

Mr F. Phillips entertains the holiday-makers on Southend beach, east of the pier, 1892. The drawing is by Arthur Rackham (*from the John Kennedy Melling Theatre Collection*)

*Left:*
Blackpool's Victoria Pier was one of the main venues for pierrot and concert party troupes

The Palace Pier, Brighton

The West Pier, Brighton, in 1914. Brighton boasted an enormous amount of beach and pier entertainment

*Right:*
'Mr Punch' as a pierrot (from the holiday pages of *Punch*, July 1914)

7

because of their permanent bow legs; and pianists whose detachable cuffs would leave their arms as they raced up and down the keyboard as they occasionally went into a faster tempo for fear of their audience drifting into a permanent sleep.

The seaside was now becoming a must for everybody. The cotton workers were pouring into Blackpool to taste the good life. Brighton had already got a head start because of the Prince Regent's assurance that the sea there was the answer to all ailments.

Some form of regular beach entertainment was required. The customers were there and the majority had a few shillings to spare. Nathaniel Hawthorne, in his English notebooks of 1857, referred to '. . . the Wandering Minstrels, with guitar and voice . . .'. Christy's Minstrels first appeared in Southport in 1860, and at this time the nigger minstrels were establishing themselves on the sands in no uncertain manner. The Moore and Burgess troupe, which included the Francis Brothers and David Day, and the Mohawk Minstrels,

which included Harry Hunter, were very popular. The Francis Brothers, Day and Hunter eventually combined to form the music publishing firm of Francis, Day and Hunter. The area on the beach in which the minstrels performed was called a 'nigger ring': a round, low-boarded enclosure like a circus ring with a small entrance for the patrons. Of course, many people would stand outside the ring or sit up on the promenade wall rather than pay their pennies for stepping over the two-foot high barrier. This situation had to be countered and so 'bottling' was introduced. One member of the company, or perhaps two, who were not engaged on the 'platform' if there was one (in many cases there wasn't) would circulate among the bystanders outside the ring and collect what they could. A good bottler was worth his weight in gold. The 'bottle' was introduced because once the money had dropped into it, it was virtually impossible to get it out until the bottle was broken in front of the whole troupe at the end of the performance.

Uncle Bones's Margate Minstrels in the 1880s
(*Kent County Library*)

Minstrels on Margate beach.
A drawing by M. Griffen-
hagen from *Picture World*,
5 August 1882 (*Kent County
Library*)

A pitch on Southport beach,
1899 (*Sefton Library and
Art Services*)

Alderman's Eastbourne
Minstrels, about 1900

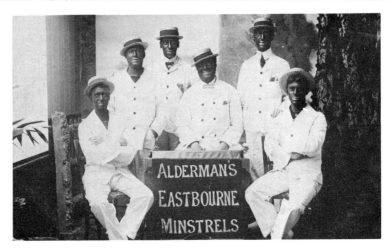

Probably one of Catlin's early troupes at
Bournemouth

CHIRGWIN'S
CONCERT PARTY

G. H. Chirgwin's concert party, 1908.
Chirgwin later made a big name for himself
as the 'White-eyed Kaffir'

The minstrels' entertainment always took the same form: members of the troupe sat in the half circle—with a comedian at each end. A dignified performer with a big speaking voice sat in the centre. He was addressed as Mr Interlocutor, and was the straight man to the comedians and compere of the programme. Many minstrels later made names for themselves on the 'halls'— Eugene Stratton, Little Tich, G. H. Elliott, G. H. Chirgwin (the 'White-eyed Kaffir').

It seemed as though nothing would dislodge the nigger minstrels from their position of popularity. But in 1890, without any fanfare of trumpets and away from the seaside, an avalanche started which swept the minstrels aside —the Pierrots. Solo minstrels continued, a few successfully: one who became UNCLE to thousands of children over the years was Uncle Mack (J. H. Summerson) at Broadstairs. Children returning to the resort year after year would immediately on arrival go down to the beach to see 'their Uncle'. Uncle Mack started by busking on the sands at Herne Bay in the early 1890s. He moved to Broadstairs beach, near the jetty, in 1895 and stayed there without a break until 1938. There is, in fact, a plaque at Broadstairs to commemorate this great man's place in Broadstairs' entertainment

An early poster for a 'Bright, New, Novel, Refined Entertainment'

C.41030. COWES, I.O.W. THE PIER.

The revolution in beach and summer entertainment that ousted the minstrels so dramatically in 1890 was started by a small group of concert singers, favourites at the Queen's and Albert Halls, who earned large fees from engagements in the homes of the well-to-do; they also performed at houseboat parties on the Thames and on yachts at Cowes. They decided not to use their own names as this might have affected their professional standing in their concert work. They wore masks and called themselves The Marguerites. At that time they wore traditional evening dress.

Early in 1891 a singer and banjoist, Clifford Essex, after a visit to France, was so taken with the costumes and make-up of *pierrot* that he had seen, that he decided to form a 'party' of pierrot entertainers, which he did. He obtained a booking at Bray near Dublin. Southern Ireland was then still part of the British Isles, so 1891 was the year that pierrot came into being in the British Isles. Essex soon established his pierrot troupe when his little party went to Cowes in the Isle of Wight for Regatta week. Cowes was at that time (and still is) the playground of the yachting fraternity. As with Epsom and Ascot weeks, Cowes was one of the main events on the social calendar, particularly because it was always patronised, to his great enjoyment, by the Prince of Wales, later Edward VII. Essex arranged his Cowes visit to coincide with Regatta week in the hope of elevating his pierrot troupe to greater respectability. Little did he imagine that he would actually perform in front of 'the Prince'. After this, Essex was allowed to call his troupe the Royal Pierrots. This title was to be bestowed at a later date on yet another 'party'.

Cowes had 'almost become a court, not just another resort'.

The newspaper *The Variety Theatre* said: 'Pierrot became the order of the day. The tasteful white costume of loose blouse, ornamented with pom-poms, the equally loose pantaloons, the natty shoe, and the black silk handkerchief which wound artistically round the head, and

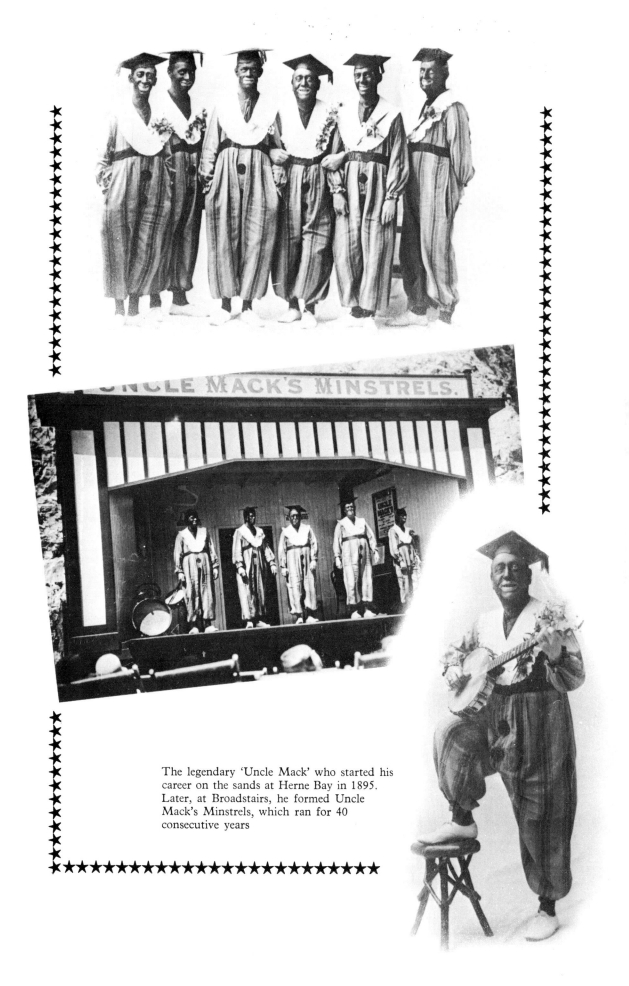

The legendary 'Uncle Mack' who started his career on the sands at Herne Bay in 1895. Later, at Broadstairs, he formed Uncle Mack's Minstrels, which ran for 40 consecutive years

tied tastefully at the side, and surmounted by the conically-shaped white hat fairly "caught on".'

Many years later Essex opened a musical instrument and publishing company in Bond Street that became famous all over the world.

When sea bathing first became fashionable during the reigns of George III and George IV, it was mostly the gentry and nobility who went to Brighthelmstone (the original name of Brighton), Weymouth and similar resorts for their health. They took to the sea like ducks to water. (The healing properties of the sea could hardly be called just water.) In fact some of them even went so far as to drink the wretched stuff! The daily dip was performed with the utmost care and attention to ritual, and Martha Gunn, a famous 'dipper' of Brighton, was accorded the greatest respect as it was she who 'dipped' His Royal Highness. When she was buried at the Parish Church of St Nicholas, thousands turned out to mourn her.

But in the 1890s bathing was not only considered beneficial for the health but was also 'found to be fun'. Yes, ordinary people were enjoying themselves in the sea. No mixed bathing of course. Bathing machines, of which there were now an abundance at resorts all over the British Isles, were segregated and it was a daring gentleman who tried to swim into the ladies' area. One can imagine the giggles of delight should a gentleman be adventurous enough to do this.

It was now the thing to make the annual pilgrimage to the seaside, and cheap rail excursions made it possible for everyone to enjoy themselves 'beside the seaside'. Southport, for instance, reported in 1897, according to F. G. Warne, 'That as many as 100,000 people had flocked into the town in a single day and a goodly proportion of these would naturally seek the pleasures of the beach'.

Clifford Essex had really started something. Will C. Pepper (who began his career with Essex) formed his own troupe, the 'White Coons', in 1899, playing seasons at Hove on the lawns (he must have had some influence in that resort, as at that time anywhere but the sands was forbidden territory for entertainers). He also went at a later date to Clacton on the east coast. (Stanley Holloway began his career with the 'White Coons'.) Will Pepper's son, Harry S. Pepper, became a well-known radio producer in the 1930s and was responsible for, amongst other shows, 'Monday Night at Eight'—compered by Ronnie Waldman who became Head of Light Entertainment BBC/TV in the '50s—and the 'Kentucky Minstrels' (the 'Black and White Minstrels' was really the TV version of this).

---

*'The flies are a bit thick in this place' I said to the landlady. 'What do you expect for a pound a day?' she said 'Educated ones?'*

The 'Cosy Nook' at Newquay, now rebuilt and enlarged. The actor Naunton Wayne – a conjuror in those days – was with the Ronald Frankau troupe which played several seasons here

The promenade at Weymouth where Edwin Adeler started

'Now, mind, if any of those nasty people with cameras come near, you're to send them away!'
(*Punch*, September 1901)

# EDWIN ADELER

Two men in particular played an enormous part in the future of pierrot, and dominated the summer entertainment scene for many, many years after humble beginnings in the mid 1890s: Edwin Adeler and Will Catlin.

Edwin Adeler, the son of a Presbyterian Minister, had already had some theatrical experience with a fit-up company. He joined forces with an entertainer called W. G. Sutton and in 1894 they decided to go to Weymouth to try their luck as seaside entertainers. They took a pianist into their partnership, hired a piano which they mounted on a trolley, and wandered up and down the prom giving their entertainment. Bottling was, of course, the only means of income. They then moved on to Harrogate, donned pierrot costumes and whitened-up with what was to become the traditional recipe, zinc and lard.

In 1898 Adeler and Sutton went to Southport, taking on another partner, a baritone, and charmed a wealthy widow into letting them perform on the front lawn of her large house adjacent to the front. They called themselves the 'Southport Pierrots', and enrolled yet another artiste, a comedian called Frank Lynne (actor Clive Dunn's grandfather). They then went to New Brighton for a season and made that their headquarters.

At about this time they met Julian Samuelson—who later changed his name to Julian Wylie. He was a great patron of Adeler and Sutton and suggested that they change the name of their troupe to the Adeler–Sutton Pierrots.

Incidentally, Julian Wylie later teamed up with a man called Tate and not only did they present their own pierrot companies but also produced several West End plays and musicals.

Tom Kelly's Southport Pierrots, 1907 (*Sefton Library and Art Services*)

VISITOR (to Percy of the 'Mauve Merriments'): 'What would you charge to sing "It's a Long Way to Tipperary" into auntie's ear-trumpet?' (*Punch*, 1914)

The home of Adeler and Sutton's pierrots

Eventually by the early 1900s, Adeler and Sutton had twenty resident pitches. (The word 'pitch' is still used today to describe a theatre or place of live entertainment at the seaside.) The enormous and rapid growth of the Adeler and Sutton empire was to cause its downfall.

During the winter, summer artistes used to come to London in the hope of obtaining after-dinner concert work. On one of Adeler's trips to London, he met up with a gentleman called Fred Raines, who was something in the City. Raines, to eke out his salary and because he rather fancied himself as an entertainer, was also performing at the odd smoking concert. He also used to take in theatrical lodgers at his house in Brixton. His son was then fourteen and worked as a call boy at the Haymarket Theatre. The boy later became the world famous screen and stage star—Claude Raines.

In these early stages of the pierrot business, the members were all male. The main reason for this being that they had a terrific following with the ladies and, even if a pierrot was married, his manager—the proprietor of the show—would make sure that this was not known in the town. Gwen Adeler, Edwin's daughter, who had a long career in the summer show business told me that to the best of her knowledge her father was the first person to employ a female artiste in a pierrot party. Adeler's new recruit was Ethel Stanhope, a beautiful young thing. Ethel eventually married Whit Cunliffe who himself was a wonderful entertainer, always immaculately dressed and a darling of the ladies. Cunliffe eventually went on to the West End and played several seasons at the Alhambra.

Adeler felt he had achieved all he had wanted in this country. He had been a very powerful influence in the summer entertainment business. He was the first person to pay Bransby Williams £100 a week, and that was in 1908. He had given a lot of people their first opportunity and enjoyed himself into the bargain.

In 1909, Adeler gave up all his interests in this country—his daughter Gwen said he had just got itchy feet and wanted to travel—and took a pierrot company to South Africa. This was the first such company to appear on the Continent of Africa. Before he went to South Africa, he gave the majority of his business to Fred Allandale, Billy Burke's husband. Fred (Bobby) Allandale was a most respected member of the profession and later became a big favourite in Blackpool. Billy Burke became a great musical comedy star and later re-married the great American impresario Florenz Ziegfeld. On Adeler's South African tour he took his daughter Gwen, who was now becoming a very good performer, and Dolly Summers. Later Dolly became the well known Dorothy Summers who played Mrs Mopp in the extraordinarily successful ITMA radio series with Tommy

Handley, who, by the way, had been a successful concert party artiste in his earlier days.

While in South Africa, Adeler started the first theatrical newspaper in South Africa, *The Stage and Cinema*. Gwen, his daughter, came back from South Africa in 1919 having married there and went into a show at Llandudno—the last venue her father had played before going to South Africa.

Gwen had started in the business, as so many others had, as a 'chairwarmer' —this involved just sitting and looking pretty for the audience. In the mid-1920s, Gwen was engaged by Wylie Tate for their show at the Central Pier, Blackpool. You may remember that Julian Wylie had been a fan of the original Adeler and Sutton Pierrots at Southport and New Brighton. Edwin Adeler eventually went on from South Africa to tour Ceylon. While there he felt his party, which now included a band led by Adeler's talented musician son, needed another young female performer. He auditioned several and eventually chose one—Queenie Thompson. She eventually changed her name and went on to become one of the very big movie stars of our age, Merle Oberon.

One interesting incident that Adeler witnessed in this country happened one evening during a Water Rats Ball at Horners Hotel, Kennington, South London. Dr Crippen was there with Ethel Le Neve. The great music hall star Marie Lloyd was present and said to a friend 'Ethel Le Neve is wearing all Bel Elmore's (Crippen's wife) jewellery'. Bel was a famous actress of the day. This scrap of information, a result of Marie Lloyd's observation, was passed on to the police who paid Crippen a visit. This was the start of an investigation that eventually led to the arrest of Crippen and Ethel Le Neve on board ship to Canada.

Lottie Mellor
Frank Cotton
Herbert Barrington
Sam Dalton

Charles Clark
Ted O'Grady
Will Styles
Will Ford

Catlin's Royal Pierrots, Whitley Bay, 1906, and at Southend in the same year. Their performances were popular at inland venues during the winter (*far right*)

THE ORIGINAL SOUTHEND PIERROTS, 1906.
East Parade Bandstand.

# WILL CATLIN

The other man, besides Edwin Adeler, who was to dominate the summer scene for so long was Will Catlin. Originally, William Fox from Leicester, Catlin saw the possibility of making a fortune out of seaside entertainment. The difference between Adeler and Catlin was that Catlin remained satisfied once he had built his empire and enjoyed keeping it going as long as it was making money, which it did for overy sixty years.

Will Catlin came on the scene in 1894 at Scarborough. His first pitch was on the sands under the Spa Wall. The Spa at Scarborough is now, and has been for some years, the summer 'home' of Max Jaffa and his Orchestra, and Eric Ross's 'Dazzle' Company. Catlin was a very

firm 'Governor'. His troupe was doing three shows a day, sometimes four. The conditions that many troupes performed in were, to say the least, poor. High winds, sometimes swirling sand, frequently rain—at times quite heavy. In a heavy rainstorm the audience would vanish or shelter under the promenade wall. The pierrots could not run across the sands for shelter, so they would huddle together on their little platform, as if in a rugby scrum, to stop their make-up from running. If the weather looked as if it was going to be bad for any length of time, their little notices would appear on, or near, the pitches announcing 'If wet under the pier'. In later years, concert parties used to

*This drunk was standing at the end of the pier, watching an angler trying to land a big 'un, when the angler lost his balance and fell in. 'I can't swim!' he shouted. 'I can't swim!' The drunk leaned over the edge and said: 'I can't play the piano, but I'm not shouting about it.'*

announce 'If wet in the Town Hall' or, as used to happen at Brighton on Madeira Drive, 'If wet in the public convenience': it must have been a very large one!

In these circumstances and under the conditions in which the pierrots had to work, it says a lot for Will Catlin's determination that he became the 'Governor' of his world. He would insist on his pierrots dressing and making up in their digs and walking down to the beach. This was a publicity gimmick that always worked. On change-over day, Saturday, when the holiday makers were leaving the town and the new ones coming in, Catlin would parade his pierrots round the town during the morning, paying several visits to the station in the course of the tour.

Catlin used to rehearse his troupe nearly every morning in a stable in the town. His pierrots really had a film star following. The rent that the Scarborough Corporation wanted for his pitch went up and up as Catlin did better and better. Because of the rises in his rental, Catlin decided to purchase a plot of land on the foreshore and build a pavilion called Arcadia. This was quite a lavish pavilion without a permanent roof. In fact, it later had a roof that could be pulled right over the top of the structure, rather like the hood over an open car. As he progressed, Catlin bought more ground and then built the first super cinema in the country, which he called 'The Futurist'. This building was the first venue played by the Black and White Minstrels when it was transferred from television to the live stage for the first time.

Catlin also bought a site in Llandudno for £400, just in front of the Grand Theatre, which was, incidentally, used for radio broadcasts during the 1939–45 war. On this site, Catlin built a pavilion which he also named Arcadia. As his

Brighton, 1924

*Opposite, top:* Easter & Vernon's Brighter Brighton Concert Party, 1924; *centre and below:* two of Catlin's troupes, 1912. The company included Tom Braham-Fox, Will Catlin's brother

UNCLE HARRY    VEDA WARDMAN    LESLIE STACEY    NELLIE BANKS

EASTER VERNONS "BRIGHTER BRIGHTON" CONCERT OCT 1924

CATLIN'S ROYAL PIERROTS

productions got bigger through the '20s, '30s and '40s, so his following became enormous. He eventually titled his productions 'Catlin's Showtime'. He also owned the Arcadia, Colwyn Bay and retired to live in Llandudno until he died at the age of 80.

Early in the reign of Edward VII, Catlin's pierrots were commanded to Ruthin Castle in Wales where the King was staying. As a result of this one night stand, Catlin's billing became 'Catlin's Royal Pierrots'; the second company to use the word 'Royal' in their title. One of Catlin's pierrots' great fans at Scarborough was the late Charles Laughton—before he became an actor. Laughton's family owned a hotel until quite recently in Scarborough. Laughton himself could be seen day after day watching his favourite pierrots.

Through the years from the early 1900s, Catlin also had touring parties playing Bridlington, Bournemouth and Yarmouth. His brother, Braham-Fox, was his manager in many of these productions and also contributed as a very good performer. He later ran his own company.

One of Catlin's daughters (Gladys) married a superb female impersonator —at one time there had been no female artistes in the pierrot shows. This particular female impersonator was Billie Manders. He worked for Catlin for some time and then took over the Amphitheatre at Rhyl in 1921 and called his production 'The Quaintesques'.

Bill Ellis of Rhyl told me about Manders. Right from the start the show was a hit. 'The Quaintesques' entertained thousands and thousands of holiday makers during its unbroken twenty-nine years' run.

It requires a great deal of art and no little histrionic skill to make the role of female impersonator absolutely un-offensive and acceptable to a critical audience: Billie Manders certainly had that skill. In 1934, 'The Quaintesques' was adjudged the best concert party in the British Isles in the *Sunday Dispatch* competition, a prize previously won by his tutor Will Catlin. In both cases the prize money was shared out among the company.

At Billie Manders' funeral in 1950, it was estimated that approximately 1500 people were present to pay their last tribute to a fellow townsman who had won the affectionate regard of all.

Britain had adopted a much more light-hearted attitude to life during the 1900s. Perhaps the new King Edward VII had something to do with this. He loved the social life and took a great interest in the theatre as a whole. Perhaps his association with Lillie Langtry had something to do with this. Anyhow, Britain, oblivious of the gathering storm, was enjoying itself in a carefree way that it had not done before. There were now hundreds of touring concert parties, not only around the seaside but also inland.

Concert parties at that stage changed the image of the pierrot show slightly. The first half would still be played in the traditional costume, but in the second half the company would wear a different type of uniform—perhaps blazers and yachting caps, or evening dress with top hats. Whatever the dress, it was always smart, clean as a whistle, and would be inspected by the proprietor before the day started. The ladies (who had now come on the scene in large numbers) had to whiten their shoes every morning and if any artiste showed slackness three days running, he, or she, would be booted out and that was that. This discipline was maintained by some managements into the 1960s.

The new wave of optimism and joyfulness—for a proportion of the population anyway—also brought the

Algy More (*far left*) in the
Playtime Follies at the Palace
Pier, St Leonards on Sea –
the site is now a swimming
pool

The new look: blazers and
boaters here have replaced
the traditional costumes

The eccentric Reuban More, father of Algy More, is standing centre

Reuban More again. On the left is Bobby Dunn – father of Clive Dunn. Reuban had troupes at Ventnor and Ryde

July 1914: the first of three fires on South Parade Pier, Southsea

SOUTH PARADE PIER, SOUTHSEA, ON FIRE, JULY 19, 1904. *Barkshire Bros., Photo., 233 Albert Rd., Southsea*

28

'Seaside minstrel, suspected of being an alien, is made to remove the black from his face for purposes of identification.' (*Punch*, 1914)

eccentrics into the business. One of these was a gentleman called Reuban More. His son Algy, now over eighty and with a very funny sense of humour himself, talked to me about his father. Reuban More started as a Company Manager, lyricist and songwriter with Adeler and Sutton at New Brighton, Southport and Tynemouth. Before the 1914–18 war he started his own company and eventually had three or four. He was then living at Southsea and took a pitch beside the Clarence Pier which is now the Hoverport base for the Isle of Wight. In this show he had a boy singer, G. H. Elliott; later G.H., as he was known, became a bill topper all over the country. Another man who started with Reuban—then as a conjurer—later became a world-famous 'vent', Arthur Prince.

More liked eccentric people around him. One day, during a matinée at Southsea, his pianist, Moses Mudd,

suddenly got up from the keyboard in the middle of the soprano's aria and said: 'I've got the call, I'm going to join the Salvation Army.' He got up, walked down the aisle among the patrons and was never heard of again. This amused More rather than annoyed him.

Reuban also played seasons on Boscombe Pier but at first the business was not good. Every morning he used to ride on the open-top trams with his vent doll 'Tinker' (Reuban appears to have been a jack of all trades) and entertained the children by speaking to them through the doll. The trams eventually became packed with children and, as a result, so did Boscombe Pier. Nobody ever did well at the venue after Reuban left. He also pulled stunts when he had the Pavilion at Ryde Pierhead. (Incidentally, the building is no longer there, but the Pier itself is, of course.)

Business was bad, so he paid a man a few shillings to jump off the pier one

afternoon during a matinée and feign drowning. This was to coincide with Reuban's baritone singing of 'On with the motley' in full regalia. At a given signal Reuban shouted 'man overboard', at which point he dashed off the stage, dived into the sea and saved the drowning man. It made news in all the local papers on the Island and in the Portsmouth evenings. This turned the business and Reuban eventually made a lot of money at this date. After this he took the Paddock Gardens, Guildford, adjacent to the site of the Yvonne Arnaud Theatre. He left the family at Southsea and took lodgings in Guildford. The house still stands just around the corner from the Co-operative store next to a church. He used to pay the company out every Friday in a most unusual way. The artistes used to have to queue up underneath his first-floor window and he would lower their wages down in an envelope, inside his slipper which was on the end of a string. The slipper would go up and down until the whole company was paid. Reuban would then go back to bed, generally to compose more music, or think of more eccentric things to annoy people with.

The German street bands were a common feature of those days and when Reuban had finished writing an arrangement, he would lean out of the

Pierrot costumes were frequently used by political cartoonists (Lords Lansdowne, Halsbury, Londonderry and Curzon; *Punch*, December 1909)

window and invite the german band, for a few shillings, into his bedsitter ('combined chat' as they were until recently generally called). The landlady nearly had him out on more than one occasion when she found six musicians in one room playing hell for leather, and Reuban lying in bed shouting 'Wonderful, wonderful, this is most eccentric'.

In his show at Guildford he had a red-nosed comic called Gillie Potter who later became a big radio star as a sophisticated comedian with his catch-phrase 'Good evening, England: this is Gillie Potter here speaking to you in English'. Potter was also a great authority on heraldry. He died recently at a ripe old age in Bournemouth.

Reuban also did seasons at Ventnor in the Isle of Wight, where his principal male artiste was Bobby Dunn, father of Clive Dunn.

Reuban created the fictitious 'Bods': a company of weird creatures who, he said, were the spirits of the actual performers. Many people in the theatre became involved with the Bods. Even in recent times there are people, such as actress Beryl Reid, who know 'all about the Bods'.

By 1910, with George V on the throne, war with Germany was getting closer but most people were ignorant of the danger, mainly because they didn't think the royal relatives in Germany and Russia (and in fact scattered all over Europe) would be so silly as to become so belligerent that they would actually want to fight one another. After all 'Teddy', although he had just died, had always kept the peace and why shouldn't his son George do the same. It was in this mood that people were still flocking to the seaside and paying their usual attention to the pierrots. But at about this time the uniform dress of the 'Boss's' choice was starting to take over in a small way from the pierrot costume. The 'parties' were also beginning to tour the inland dates, but not until later did this become the norm rather than the unusual.

The Fol-de-Rols in the early 1920s. Clive Dunn's mother, Connie Clive, is sitting far right in the front row

GEORGE ROYLE'S MERRY IMPS.

THE "Will o' the Wisps" SPA THEATRE.

One of George Royle's companies. He also had the 'Imps' and later the famous Fol-de-Rols. He started in Blackpool before his move to Scarborough and other resorts in association with Greatrex Newman

The 'Will o' the Wisps' and the 'Merry Imps': two of George Royle's companies prior to the Fol-de-Rols

# THE 'FOL-DE-ROLS'

About 1910, in some resorts, there were as many as three or four beach parties in operation at the same time, in addition to solo buskers and entertainers.

George Royle had a show called 'The Imps' on the South sands at Scarborough, having previously run 'The Troubadors' at Blackpool. This 'Imps' company included Jack Waller, who later joined Herbert Clayton as Clayton and Waller, and presented *No No Nanette* and other big musicals. Mark Daly, who became a West End musical comedian, was also an 'Imp'.

The Scarborough Corporation had just opened their new Floral Hall—which still accommodates summer shows today—with a concert party that unfortunately folded in early August, so the Corporation asked Royle to transfer his 'Imps' from the sands to finish the season indoors at the new building. The move was a success, and Royle was offered the Floral Hall for the next season, 1911.

The Hall was of the large green-house type then fashionable—similar to the original Winter Gardens at Bournemouth, with hanging floral baskets and rockeries of attractive flowering plants—and Royle felt this setting demanded rather more dignified costumes than the pierrot variation then worn by the 'Imps'. The building had a rather Victorian garden party atmosphere, so the ladies of the 1911 company were dressed in charming crinolines and bonnets, and the men in coloured frock coats and trousers, lace jabots and silk toppers. But the name 'Imps' seemed incongruous with this more sedate attire, so Royle christened them the 'Fol-de-Rols'—suggested by the old English song 'Fol-de-de-rol laddie'.

The Follies who performed at Sandringham for Queen Alexandra's birthday

SOUTH BAY, SCARBOROUGH.

Scarborough, where many famous troupes began: including the Fol-de-Rols, Catlin's Pierrots and later Catlin's Showtime

This enlarged and more ambitious show was so successful that they were re-booked in 1912–13–14, though the war emptied Scarborough in August 1914 when two German warships bombarded Hartlepool. But the 'Fols' played on until the end of September, which was financially disastrous for Royle with no visitors in the town.

At the end of the war in November 1918, the corporation offered Royle the tenancy at a much increased rental, but —having lost heavily in 1914 and with post-war prospects uncertain—he felt he needed a partner to share in the venture. He mentioned this to a concert party agent through whom he had previously booked artistes, and the agent thereupon suggested to a recently demobbed pilot, Greatrex Newman, that this seemed a good investment for his RAF gratuity—with the result that

the 1919 'Fol-de-Rols' were presented by the newly-formed management of George Royle and Greatrex Newman.

Newman had spent two pre-war summers with the 'Gems', but was more interested in writing than performing. He had always been an avid lover of summer entertainment since he'd been taken at an early age to the Central Pier at Blackpool to see Bobby Allandale's show, which included a great seaside favourite, Fred Walmsley.

Royle produced the 'Fol-de-Rols' and appeared in the show, while Newman wrote original material and kept an eye on the box office. The new 'Fols' became more and more successful as season followed season.

The Hastings Corporation built the White Rock Pavilion in 1926 and invited

. . . and so many performers joined ENSA. This notice was posted at the Theatre Royal, Brighton, where Jim Hunter's Brighton Follies had moved after the Palace Pier closed on 1 September 1939

No doubt about who is the comic: Varda the white make-up

Tom Howell's 'Opieros', around 1929. (Their programmes always included scenes from popular operas, hence the rather strange name)

the 'Fol-de-Rols' for the opening season. They successfully remained in residence there each summer until the Second War closed the Pavilion in 1939.

At this time Rex Newman was also writing material for London shows. He was under contract to supply material for the famous 'Co-optimists'—David Burnaby, Phyllis Monkman, Laddie Cliff, Melville Gideon and the utility-man-cum-baritone, who was Stanley Holloway. One of their pierrots was Walsley Charles of 'The Scamps' fame. Rex Newman also wrote the London success *Mr Cinders* which ran for two years and was part-author of *Lady Luck*. He was also writing for the Vaudeville Revues and a bunch of comics called the Crazy Gang.

Before and during the war years, the Fols—*The show that any child can take its parents to!*—carried on throughout the Middle East countries, Cyprus and Malta, and then re-visited France and toured Germany following Mr Hitler's exit.

With peace restored, they returned to Scarborough, Hastings and Eastbourne and also dropped anchor at Torquay.

In 1955, Peter Donald (a director of Howard & Wyndham) saw the show while on holiday in Scarborough, and arranged for it to follow on its seaside season with four weeks at the King's Theatre, Edinburgh in October. It was so well received there that this resulted in the Fols being the Christmas attraction at that town's Lyceum Theatre the following year—and they played four to six week seasons there for each of the next seven Christmasses; their Scottish bookings being extended after the second Edinburgh year to include an annual four weeks at the King's Theatre, Glasgow, and a month at HM Theatre, Aberdeen. Latterly they spent eighteen winter weeks North of the Border each winter while still taking

The pierrot as hero – an illustration from
*Woman's World*, 1909

*It was freezing cold when I got back
to my boarding-house last night. 'Any
chance of a fire?' I asked the landlady.
'No' she said, 'There's a bucket of sand
in every room.'*

their buckets and spades to the seasides
in the summer.

The Fols had previously played a
successful winter season at the St
Martin's Theatre—with unanimous
acclaim from the West End press—and
had also been included in the Royal
Variety Performance.

I have the happiest recollections of
the two summers when I wore a Fols
top hat; and other old Fol-de-Rolians
included Arthur Askey, Richard
Murdoch, Jack Warner, Walter
Midgley (all in the Hastings 1938
company), Elsie and Doris Waters,
Western Bros, Avril Angers, Reg
Dixon, Cyril Fletcher, Doris Hare,
Bill Frazer, David Nixon and Leslie
Crowther.

There were also the backbone
performers of the Fols: they used to be
talked of as 'He's a real Fol'. They
knew exactly how the material should
be performed to get every ounce out of
it. People like Jack Tripp, an exceptional
comic and a superb dancer. Kathleen
West, who could make the telephone
directory sound funny. Cyril Wells a
comedy character actor of huge talent,
Peter Felgate who also later produced
some of the shows, and Allen Christie, an
Australian with a great knowledge of
'Fols' performing.

George Royle retired in 1935; and
Rex carried on the good work for
another twenty-five years until 1960,
when he retired and sold the show to
Jack Hylton and Jack's brother-in-law
Hugh Charles. Jack has since died,
leaving Hugh at the helm.

The 1920s saw a kind of
sophistication, if one can call it that,
creeping into the concert party at the
seaside, without losing the essential
ingredient of this type of entertainment,
which basically was simple family fare.
The resorts still had their favourite
shows and favourite entertainers.

*Above right:* the Co-Optimists, 1926
(*Radio Times Hulton Picture Library*)

"FOL-DE-ROLS" FLORAL HALL. SCARBOROUGH.

Back row, far right is Reg Lever; standing
in the centre are Elsie and Doris Waters; far
right of the middle row is George Lacy, 1930

The sun has been too much for them! Jack
Sheppard's Highwaymen at Brighton during
World War I

THE HIGHWAYMEN

Jack Sheppard's Entertainers
Season 1920

Brighton.

. . . by 1920 the troupe was renamed Jack
Sheppard's Entertainers. Max Miller made
his seaside debut with them – he was their
great 'bottler'

40

# BRIGHTON

Jack Sheppard ran a small troupe in the early 1900s in Brighton called the 'Highwaymen'. After the First World War he started a more ambitious company in Brighton called 'Jack Sheppard's Brighton Entertainers', with two pitches: one opposite the Madeira Walk very near where the London to Brighton Veteran Car Rally finishes nowadays, and one opposite the Metropole Hotel near the West Pier. Both pitches were alfresco. Sheppard was present right through the '20s and '30s. In 1919 he engaged a young light comedian just commencing his career for £2.10s a week, later rising to £3.10s a week. His name was Harry Sargent. He later, on the advice of his wife, changed his name to Max Miller and went on to become one of the greatest stand-up music hall comedians of our age. In the 1920s Max also worked in 'The Rogues' run by Fred Roper and Bart Brady, and did a season for the great concert party proprietor, Ernest Binns. Miller was not only a good concert party comedian in his early days, he was also a great 'bottler', gagging with the customers as he went round collecting.

Palace Pier, Brighton

THE CHAIN PIER IN 1838

The Chain Pier, Brighton was just a few
hundred yards east of the existing Palace
Pier. It was destroyed in a storm in 1896

The top deck of the Aquarium, Brighton,
was a concert party pitch

Opposite the Palace Pier at Brighton
is the Aquarium which was a touring
concert party date at one time. The
Palace Pier itself housed many concert
parties, including one of the most
popular in the '30s—'Jimmy Hunter's
Brighton Follies'. In small print in the
programme is the name Tommy Trinder.
That's where 'You lucky people' started.
It was at Brighton that Jack Hylton took
Tommy Trinder out of the Pier Show
and starred him at the Hippodrome in
Middle Street. This came about when
Jack Hylton, on the opening night of his
show at the Brighton Hippodrome
*Life Begins at Oxford Circus* which had
been running at the London Palladium,
went along to a local hotel to have a
drink and was advised by an acquaintance,
Sir Harry Preston, to go along to the
Palace Pier and see a comedian called
Trinder. This Jack Hylton did and
immediately signed him up for his
Hippodrome show and subsequent tour
which, incidentally, featured Mrs Jack
Hylton's Band. Tommy Trinder never
looked back after that, becoming one of
the few British stars to reach
international stardom.

# MARGATE

The Thanet area, Ramsgate, Broadstairs, Cliftonville and Margate, was a centre of summer entertainment. Arthur Askey was at Margate very early in his career with Fred Wildon's Entertainers. Leonard Henry, also to become a big radio name, was on the jetty at Margate. The brilliant light comedian Bobby Howes (whose daughter Sally Anne was later to make a name for herself in Hollywood musicals and the theatre) began his career in concert parties in this resort.

One of the big successes at Margate for a long time was an entertainer called Leslie Fuller who had a film star following in the Thanet and surrounding areas. Also popular in the resort for many years was 'Gold's Margate Pierrots' and later 'Entertainers'.

Margate was the venue for Cyril Fletcher's 'Magpie Masquerade' with a newcomer called Harry Secombe. Clive Dunn was another Margate entertainer. Bill Fraser (later to become a distinguished West End actor) had his 'Between Ourselves' company at the Westgate Pavilion—a very good company indeed.

At the Westbrook Pavilion was Ann Rogers, who later made such a hit in *My Fair Lady*. At the Lido, Reg Varney and his 'feed', Benny Hill. Terry Scott, Hugh Lloyd, John Boulter and a fabulous pianist, Jo Stewart, at the Winter Gardens. Norman Vaughan also did a season there.

Gold's Margate Pierrots, about 1912

The Troubadours on the sands at Margate

SANDS, MARGATE.

S 5211

THE OVAL

# BOURNEMOUTH

Bournemouth has had many successful shows: Birchmore and Lyndon's 'Gay Cadets' and Willie Cave's 'Revels', in particular. George Fairweather, now a successful hairdresser in the town, has many happy memories of working with Willie Cave. Bournemouth was the starting-off point for Tony Hancock (under the guidance of Fairweather). A summer revue at the Royal featured Terry Thomas and 'Monsieur' Eddie Gray. Bournemouth, of course, had become a great centre for music of all kinds. Sir Dan Godfrey had put the old Winter Gardens on the map with his fine music. Later, Bournemouth was to play host to practically every British performer of any note.

The Pavilion, Bournemouth

This was where Sir Dan Godfrey used to lead the Bournemouth Municipal Orchestra and established Bournemouth's reputation as a centre for concerts

*Left:* the Oval, Margate, in the early 1900s. This was a famous pierrot and concert party pitch. Arthur Askey appeared here in Fred Wilson's troupe; it was also the home of the legendary Margate entertainer Leslie Fuller

THE PIER, BOURNEMOUTH.

George Fairweather – who now runs a
hairdressing business in Bournemouth – and
music publisher Gerald Benson have happy
memories of being with Willie Cave's Revels
(*Bournemouth News and Picture Service*)

Willie Cave's Revels.
Bournemouth. 1932.

A venue for touring concert troupes and
resident shows, including that of Reuban More

Birchmore and Lyndon's Gay Cadets,
Bournemouth, 1924 (*Bournemouth News
and Picture Service*)

# BLACKPOOL

The Blackpool story is the same. From pierrot shows right through to all the biggest attractions that could be acquired.

One of the first pierrot troupes to appear at this resort was run by Bobby Allandale (previously with Adeler and Sutton), in the early 1900s on the Central Pier, known as the People's Pier.

Before breakfast, dancing was featured on the Central Pier. On one occasion, 250 Welsh miners asked the band to play some particular dance music, unfortunately the musicians didn't have the necessary music at hand, so the Welshmen went on the rampage! Music stands were thrown into the sea, policemen's helmets knocked off— hooliganism is nothing new!

Fred Emney was a member of Wylie Tate's Pierrots in the 1920s at Blackpool.

The South Pier, formerly The Victoria Pier, was the home of Fred Walmsley and his 'Tonics' in the early 1900s.

Later, one of Blackpool's favourites was Ernest Binns, with his long running 'Arcadian Follies'. In one company at this time was Harry Korris (known as 'Blackpool's other Tower') who went on to become famous as 'One of We Three', in radio's wartime Happidrome Show.

The Sun Lounge on the North Pier, was the home of Ernie Moss's 'Seafarers' concert party.

Blackpool, in the late 1920s and '30s started presenting big revues in the town's large capacity theatres, and the pierrots and concert parties had to fight an ever increasing battle against the more sophisticated and bigger shows, which by now starred the top names in British variety, and frequently from across the Atlantic as well: Jeannette MacDonald, Paul Robeson, Allan Jones (father of Jack—the singer, not the trades union leader!)

Many pierrot and concert party troupes performed here, mainly on the pier

Central Pier from the Entrance, Blackpool

*'Madam, is that your little boy who is burying my coat in the sand?'*
*'No, that's my friend's boy. Mine is the one sailing your hat in the sea.'*

'I had such a lovely bathe last Thursday, dear.'
'That was the day of the tidal wave, wasn't it, Auntie?'
(*Punch*, August 1906)

# THE
# ISLE OF WIGHT

The gentleman on the right of the group
inset is my father-in-law. He later went on
to star with Harry Lauder at the Shaftesbury
Theatre, London

FARE 1ᴰ

3  RYDE (Isle of Wight). — View from the Pi

The Isle of Wight has always been a paradise for holiday makers.

We have already mentioned the resorts Ryde and Ventnor, but one man more than any other was responsible for putting Shanklin on the map; his name was Powis Pinder. Talking to his son Arthur was fascinating. Powis produced a show on the Pier in 1920 only to see it burnt down early in his career. Undaunted and not wanting to lose the following he had built up in the short time he had been on the pier, Pinder bought some old seaplane sheds at Bembridge, took them apart and reconstructed them on the front at Shanklin and

— LL.

Ventnor Pier

The Pier from the Cliffs.     Shanklin.

opened his own Summer Theatre.

This was the big success of the '20s and '30s on the island. He featured Edwin Styles there for a long time. Styles went on to become a very fine West End actor. Fred Yule, later of ITMA fame, was with Styles in that show. Pinder had seen a funny little man in glasses in a touring concert party 'Song Salad' at Ventnor and engaged him to succeed the very popular Styles. This man was Arthur Askey. Arthur stayed with Pinder for eight or nine years, until he went into radio's Bandwagon. Webster Booth was in the same show and so was Bernard Lee, now well known through his film performances, particularly in the James Bond series as 'M'. Bernard was paid £11 for his first season at Shanklin; his wife, Gladys Merredew, was in the show with him. Gladys, only a few years ago, died tragically in a fire at their home in Kent.

Summer Theatre, Shanklin.

POWIS PINDER'S COMPANY

"SUNSHINE"

EVERY EVENING AT 8.15.

Margery Peck
Michael Strong
Gladys Merredew
Barbara Deames
Wilma van Dusen

Webster Booth
Kathleen O'Hagan
Bernard Lee
Nellie Furmage
and
Arthur Askey

BOOK SEATS AT THE SUMMER THEATRE, Phone 60.

Prices Including Tax  3/-  2/4  1/10  1/3.

CARS PARKED FREE IN SUMMER THEATRE GROUNDS.

Programme Changed Nightly.

**Summer Theatre, Shanklin.**

EVERY EVENING at 8.15.

Monday, Wednesday, Thursday & Saturday.

POWIS PINDER'S CO.

# "SUNSHINE"

Billie Desmond

Sheila Bickett

Fred Yule

and

Connie Crighton

Gladys Merredew

Eva Cobbett L.R.A.M.

Doreen
Montgomery

and

Teddy Styles

Tuesday, George Ellis' Co., "Joy."

With George Ellis and Charles Hayes.

Friday, Ronald Frankau's Co. "The Rag Dolls."

☞ SPECIAL PRICES for LARGE PARTIES.

Programme Changed Nightly.

Powis Pinder certainly had a genius for
talent spotting. *Left:* a poster of 1931 and
*right,* 1924

53

BOY: 'Please remember the driver.'
PASSENGER: 'You fiend! I shall *never* forget you–'

'A few artistic suggestions adapted to Modern Bathing Vans'

'Hints to beginners'

'The latest terror'

# BOGNOR REGIS

Bognor Regis in its small way boasted its entertainers. Firstly, Fred White's 'White Coons' on the beach and later on the lawns, and Uncle George and his 'Thespians' on the beach opposite the Steine.

Bognor at a later date was also Wallis Arthur's 'home' and his company included Clarkson Rose, who was later to conquer practically every seaside resort with his company 'Twinkle'. Clarkson Rose in his book *Beside the Seaside* describes how Clifford Gray, while appearing with the 'Drolls', found fame and fortune overnight, as a result of writing the hit song 'If you were the only Girl in the World', which George Robey and Violet Loraine set London alight with in the 'Bing Boys'.

Later at Bognor, Eric Ross's 'Dazzle' included a small pretty girl with a phenomenal voice called Julie Andrews. Clive Dunn, Dick Emery, myself and many others have done seasons at Bognor.

The Sands, Bognor

The Pier, Bognor

# SKEGNESS

Skegness had one of the most astute men in the business in the 1920s. His show was Fred Clement's 'Royal Entertainers'; first on the beach and lawns then later on the pier. Clements was originally a ticket clerk at Liverpool Street Station. He used to employ three of four comics in each show, an unheard of thing to do those days—a sort of forerunner of the Crazy Gang.

A comedian called Bunny Baron, who played practically every seaside resort in the country, always had ambitions to run his own shows. This he did eventually and became one of the biggest seaside show proprietors in the country. His shows have included Pearl Carr and Teddy Johnson, Tommy Trinder, Dai Francis, Don Estelle and Windsor Davies, John Hanson, Aimi MacDonald, Ian Lavender, Melvyn Hayes, Milligan and Nesbitt, and so on. Not bad for a comic who started on the beach.

The audience at Skegness, about 1911

18816 SOUTHEND, THE PIER.

# SOUTHEND

Southend boasted the longest pier in the country (the end of the pier was burnt out in 1977) and it could also boast some of the best concert parties. A comedian with whom I worked and who I thought should have made it, was the very tall, gangling Chip Sanders, a great favourite at Southend. Whatever he did was funny. Although he, and many, many like him, never made it nationally, they have the satisfaction of knowing that they used to send thousands and thousands of holiday makers home happy and with a great desire to see them again, wherever they might be appearing.

One man who had a special magic at the seaside and went on to become a big star, I remember first seeing at Babbacombe in Devon, when I was doing a season at Newquay in Cornwall. We (the company) used to hire a coach every Sunday to go over to see the Sunday performances at Babbacombe. Someone had suggested we went once but we just couldn't keep away after

the first visit. The attraction was a thin, vital man oozing charm and a great deal of talent. He used to conduct a give-away in the second half of the show. Getting people up on the stage, playing games and giving away prizes, plastic salt-cellars, packets of crisps, balloons, etc. He used to make the audience feel they'd won the moon. He would then finish the evening off playing the piano, dancing and gagging with all and sundry. It was sheer magic. That chap was Bruce Forsyth. Co-incidentally, I was doing a season two years later in the 'Fol-de-Rols' at Eastbourne and Bruce was in a similar show to the one at Babbacombe in the other theatre at Eastbourne. One wonderful night we heard that Bruce had been engaged to take over the compering job in television's 'Sunday Night at The London Paladium'. From then on his rise to fame was meteoric. No one, in my opinion, has deserved his success more than Bruce.

 *My landlady's so mean she counts the salt.*

# GORLESTON

The late '20s and '30s saw the emergence at Gorleston-on-Sea near Yarmouth of two of the most prolific writers of concert party material in the country. They had their own show called 'The Gorleston Gossips' at the Pavilion in 1928. I am certain that at some time or other every summer show performer has used material written by Bob Wilcock and Robert Rutherford. They had an uncanny knack of knowing exactly what was right for seaside audiences. In 1927 Elsie and Doris Waters took a lease on the Gorleston Pavilion with their show 'The Enthusiasts'.

Their own act then consisted of piano and violin duets. Before this, in the early '20s, Elsie and Doris were with Will Peppers' 'White Coons' at Southwold. As Gert and Daisy they made a huge radio and music hall name for themselves. What a talented family! Their brother Jack Warner, who also started in concert party was to become a big radio star in shows like *Garrison Theatre*, with his catch phrases such as 'Mind my bike' and 'My little gal' and 'My bruver Syd'. 'My little gal' was, incidentally, Charles Shadwell's daughter, Joan Winters. Shadwell of course led the BBC Variety Orchestra for many years. Jack Warner's career took in films including *The Blue Lamp* which was the jumping off ground for BBC TV's *Dixon of Dock Green* in which he starred for so many years. Jack also has a marvellous stage act which includes a very accurate impression of the late Maurice Chevalier.

'How Week-end-on-Sea looks in reality, and how it becomes transfigured by the hand of the poster artist.' (*Punch*, July 1907)

Harry Mitchell Craig also had connections with Gorleston and later Yarmouth, where he produced shows in both places. Mitchell Craig, who had spent many years in concert party, was one of the most respected producers in the summer resorts. He too, like Billie Manders, married one of Will Catlin's daughters.

In 1914, one party at the Olympia Quay Gardens in Gorleston, opposite the Pavilion, and now a swimming pool, was 'The Ad-Libs Entertainers'. The pianist for this show was Jack Hylton, later to become one of the great broadcasting, recording and stage bandleaders. Hylton also presented many lavish West End musical shows. He had a financial interest in the famous 'Fol De Rols' for a time and was a big contributor to Commercial Television when it first started. In the early 1900s Hylton had also been a pianist with other concert parties, including the 'Comedy Cameos'.

Gorleston has sentimental memories for me as I started my concert party days there at the Pavilion—and met my wife during that season. In that show was a wonderfully friendly, warm and very competent comedian called Clifford Hensley. He taught me a lot and we remained firm friends until his death just a few years ago.

Carney & West's Concert Party, Gorleston Pavilion.      Season 1906.
Sam Hilton.        Will Sutton.        Henry J. Hamlyn.        J. W. Harrison.
          Tom Carney.        Miss Bertha Floyd.        Chas. West.

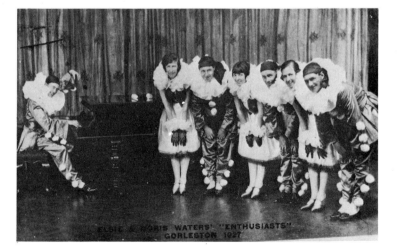

Elsie and Doris Waters' Enthusiasts – Elsie is left in line and Doris second from right. Jack Upsom is the pianist

60

# YARMOUTH

Paskin's 'Come to the Show' 1937 at the
Winter Gardens, Yarmouth. Fourth from
the left in the middle row is Jerry Desmond
– later Sid Field's straight man. In the same
row second from left is his brother, Jack
Desmond

The first Britannia Pier Pavilion, Yarmouth:
opened 21 June 1902 it was one of Catlin's
pitches, but was destroyed by fire on 22
December 1909

*Right:* Reg Maddox (centre foreground)
later took over several theatres, including the
Theatre Royal, Bath, and the Granville
Theatre, Hereford. His son, Frank, carried
on the tradition until 1976. On the left in
the back row is Chris Wortman, who made
a name for himself as the first person in
this country to do Al Jolson impersonations

Gorleston's big neighbour, Yarmouth, has become a smaller version of Blackpool. Practically every star has appeared there one way or another over the years, at the Aquarium, the Brittania Pier, Wellington Pier, Windmill Theatre and the vast open-air Marina. Neville Bishop was the Governor at the Marina—his band shows, talent contests, children's shows and beauty contests, were all conducted with great enthusiasm. I first met Neville at Yarmouth in 1955; he was an enormous success there over the years.

How strange to think that later Neville would buy a small hotel in Thetford, Norfolk, and in the bar of that hotel would be shot the first scene ever for the television series *Dad's Army*. Thetford and area was used for over nine years as the location for making *Dad's Army*.

In the '20s and '30s, both the Wellington and Brittania Piers had an enormous number of touring concert parties. At this time across the country there were something like three hundred titles (I have most of them).

In 1929, a comedian called Chris Wortman was engaged as light comedian

TED MADDOX'S EVENING FOLLIES

Photo by Sarony, Gt. Yarmouth

Britannia Pier, Great Yarmouth.

and producer of a show called 'Evening Follies' at the Wellington Pier Yarmouth, presented by Reg Maddox. Maddox was later, with his family, to lease the Theatre Royal, Bath, and a theatre at Hereford. When Maddox took over the theatre at Hereford, he started by showing films. His first film there was the first talking picture, Al Jolson's *The Jazz Singer*. They were not 'wired' for sound at the Granville at Hereford, so Maddox asked his comedian, Chris Wortman, to go and see the film in London and learn Jolson's songs. This he did, and then went down to Hereford where he joined a small orchestra in the pit and during every performance sang the Jolson songs following Jolson's

mouth movements meticulously. Normally it was fine except when the film went slower or sometimes when the projectionist ran the film faster than normal if he wanted to get home early. Wortman was also in Maddox's 1932 company. Before this he had been in the Wilcock and Rutherford party at Gorleston in 1928.

Next to the Wellington Pier, Yarmouth, in the summer of 1934, a whisky firm erected an electronic scoreboard for the whole of the Test Match series between England and Australia: the first of its kind ever to be operated in this country. What excitement watching Don Bradman's record score of 334 mount up!

*Centre left:* the second Britannia Pier Pavilion. It was opened 11 July 1910, but was again destroyed by fire in July 1914

*Below left:* 'Alfresco' 1914, on Wellington Pier, Yarmouth

The Bandstand, Wellington Gardens, Yarmouth, 1921

'Have you noticed how clean and spotless everything is at this resort?' 'I should say so. Even the seagulls fly upside down.'

65

The Cabaret Kittens at 'Cosy Nook', Newquay, early 1920s. In the centre of the front row is Naunton Wayne

With the touring concert parties in full swing it was inevitable that the inland dates played a big part in the development of artistes and shows. Ronald Frankau had 'The Blues' and 'The Cabaret Kittens' in which he featured a conjuror who later made a big name for himself in films and the West End Stage: Naunton Wayne. Wayne's partnership with Basil Radford in British comedy films became famous. Frankau, of course, later teamed up with Tommy Handley in radio and they became legendary as 'Murgatroyd and Winterbottom' and Colonel Curry and Major Rice. Incidentally, Frankau's pianist then was Monte Crick who later became the first Dan Archer on radio.

Among the cast of 'Cabaret Kittens' in 1929 was Bert Brownbill who later became an established West End actor. Pianist and comedienne Nan Kenway was also with Ronald Frankau's company. Nan later teamed up with comedian and song writer Douglas Young and they eventually became a top of the bill act in the theatre and on radio with their wartime catch phrase 'Very tasty—very sweet'. They were two of the most respected people in show business.

'Please, Mr Musician, could you play "Ta-Ra-Ra Boom-De-Ay"?' – The Trials and Tribulations of a Seaside Performer

*Right:* the Cabaret Kittens in the early 1920s, on the far left in both pictures is Ronald Frankau. In the centre picture Emilie Benfield is on the far right. *Below:* Ronald Frankau's The Blues, 1923

"Cabaret" Kittens.

Ronald Frankau          Vera Blanche          Esmé Francis          Billie Barr
        Leo Corniche          Cecil Sandrick          John Bampman

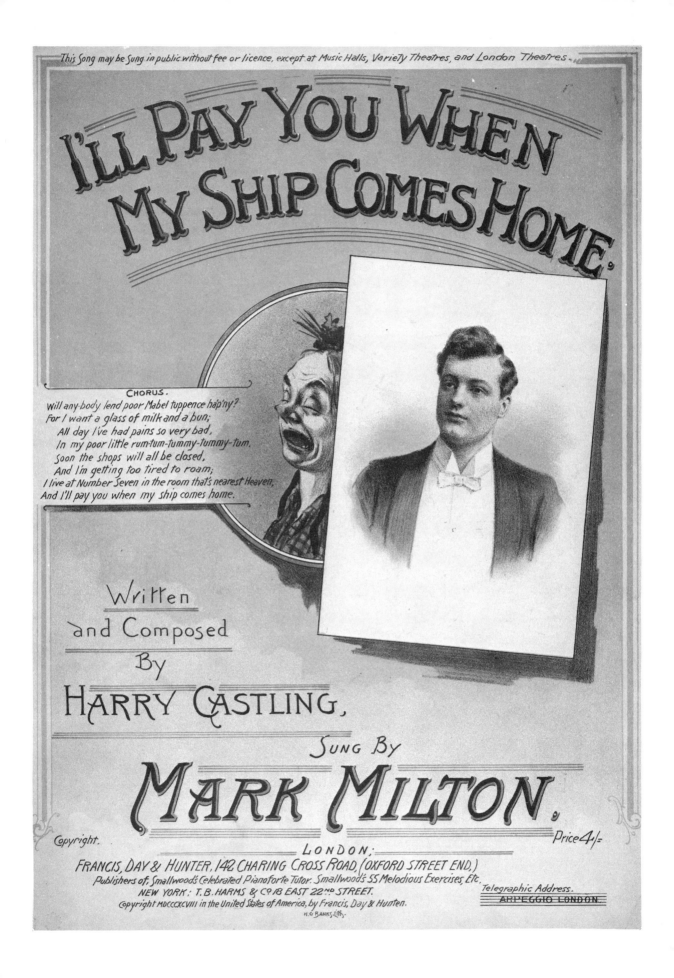

Mrs Leo Bliss' 'Busy Bees', Whitley Bay, 1925. The same troupe is pictured on the title page

Emilie Benfield, apart from being a brilliant pianist with many summer shows and personal accompanist to Ronald Frankau, Terry Thomas, Kenneth Horne and Richard Murdoch in their concert days, had a particular job to do for concert party managements. At the start of a performance her immediate task during the opening chorus was to cast her eyes along the line of gentlemen to see if their dress was properly adjusted. I played several seasons with Emilie and she never wavered from this responsibility.

A troupe at Weston-super-Mare, a regular touring date for pierrots – their pitch was near the Knightstone Pavilion (*Bournemouth News and Picture Service*)

Leslie Henson was with Wolsley Charles's 'Scamps' at the Rusholme Pavilion, Manchester, when he was seen by George Grossmith and brought to London to star at the 'Gaiety' at the top of the Strand. Henson went on to become one of the biggest names in the London Theatre. Leslie's son, Nicky, is now a well-known stage and film personality. Claude Hulbert came down from Cambridge and was engaged for Ernest Crampton's 'Cigarettes'. Later Claude teamed up with his wife Enid Trevor, his brother Jack Hulbert (also a Cambridge man) and Jack's wife Ciceley Courtnidge. All four went on to become big names in the theatre and films.

David Burnaby also came down from Cambridge and formed the 'March Hares' Concert Party. Burnaby, along with Leslie Henson, started the incredibly successful 'Co-optimists'. Who would have thought that a pierrot show would take London by storm and run for over six years in the West End. There was 'Pelliser's Follies' used, as others were, as curtain raisers in the straight theatre in London. They would do a twenty-minute excerpt before the play started. Pelliser married one of his young follies who became a big name in the theatre: Fay Compton.

When Leslie Henson was playing at Teignmouth in a show on the end of the pier, he had a sketch which required a big bang. On the opening night he put a small maroon in a dustbin for this purpose. The lifeboat crew were not told about it and when they heard the enormous explosion, all rushed to the boat and put to sea.

The whole of the North East Coast had concert parties: Tynemouth, South Shields, Hartlepool, Sunderland (Roker), Whitley Bay and Newbiggin. Billy Dodds was a great favourite in the North East.

The Yorkshire coast, apart from Scarborough, which I've already mentioned, had Whitby, Bridlington and Filey as their other main attractions. It was in the Yorkshire area that most of the touring concert parties did well inland; Harehills Pavilion, Leeds, and Bradford amongst them. Bradford started a chain of events for two people in particular, that was to make them popular in their different ways.

Ben Popplewell, who was working in a solicitor's office in Bradford, decided to go into concert party. He learnt what he could very quickly and then started a company called 'The Good Companions'. He acquired the Frizinghall Pavilion on the outskirts of the town and very soon his Good Companions had a very big following, among them J. B. Priestley who used to go and watch his shows regularly. Priestley eventually wrote a book about a touring company and called it *The Good Companions*. If J. B. Priestley was a fan of Popplewell's show, so too were many more—not only in Bradford but also at Ayr in Scotland, where Popplewell eventually moved. He bought the Gaiety there and, with his family, made

The author on the site of the Frizinghall Pavilion, Bradford, at one time a famous inland venue. Ben Popplewell had his own company here: The Good Companions. J. B. Priestley, a frequent visitor to the show, based his book of the same name on a group of touring players

*Left:* the Avonmores, about 1919 – a gay little bunch!

'Does it ever rain here?'
'Rain? . . . I've seen five-year-old frogs in this town that haven't learnt to swim yet.'

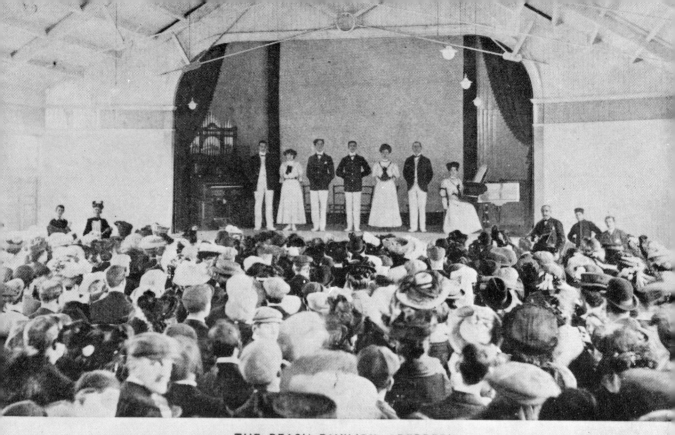

THE BEACH PAVILION, ABERDEEN.

this one of the most successful venues in the British Isles. Hundreds and hundreds of artistes appeared there in the Gaiety Revues and millions of patrons have seen his shows over the years. His two sons ran it after Ben's death and they finally sold it to the local authority, but it still boasts the same high standard of summer show.

Apart from some other smaller popular venues in Scotland, Aberdeen was perhaps the most talked about. The Beach Pavilion, Aberdeen, with its governor, Harry Gordon—or perhaps a better word would be 'father'—has only to be mentioned to a performer and he or she will say 'I've played there with Harry' or 'I know someone who was at the Beach Pavilion'. Harry not only generated an atmosphere of well-being to the customers but also to all the artistes he employed. The between-show tea parties in Harry's dressing room will be remembered by many performers. Many of today's big names worked at the Beach Pavilion, Aberdeen.

This photograph dates from about 1917, before the great Harry Gordon took over the Beach Pavilion and made it his own with many of today's big names in his company

Before Harry took over the Beach Pavilion, a female ventriloquist became the darling of Aberdeen in the early 1900s. Maude E. Edwards was a beautiful girl, young and very talented. Her whole family were connected with the Beach Pavilion. She went all over the world conquering audiences wherever she went. When Miss Edwards retired she went to Brainsworth Home, the home for professional performers at Twickenham. On her seventieth birthday she was given the honour of presenting the Queen Mother with a bouquet on a royal visit.

73

# THE BIG HEAVY SWELL OF THE SEA.

*The fellows look upon me with a jealouse eye,*
*The ladies all adore me as I saunter by,*
*They titter and they blush, then after me they rush,*
*The heviest of heavy seaside swells am I.*

WRITTEN BY
## T. L. CLAY

SUNG WITH THE GREATEST SUCCESS BY

COMPOSED BY
## ALFRED LEE.

# GEORGE LEYBOURNE.

LONDON: CHARLES SMEARD, 192, HIGH HOLBORN, W. C.

To one particular person, the word seaside must indeed be a magic word: Billy Butlin. If seaside was a magic word for him then Butlins has been something quite magic for millions of holidaymakers and hundreds and hundreds of entertainers, or would-be entertainers. Billy Butlin—now Sir Billy—built an enormous empire of entertainment round our coasts from very small beginnings. When Butlin was a seaside amusement operator in the 1930s, he realised that the British public needed something more than just a boarding house holiday. When it rained, which was and still is quite often, holiday makers had to walk round the resort getting wetter and wetter and getting more bored as the week or fortnight wore on. It was general practice for the landladies not to want, in most cases not allow, their guests back into their boarding houses during the day. After breakfast, it was all out until high tea at 5 pm. (They never did lunches.) Before irate boarding house proprietors lynch me, let me say that there were, of course, exceptions.

Billy Butlin felt sorry for the people when he saw them, grown-ups and children alike, walking around trying to make the best of the weather or looking for somewhere to go indoors. He also realised he could probably make money out of their problem if he could think of an answer to it. He found the answer and he certainly deserved to make money out of it.

Butlin opened his first holiday camp at Skegness in 1936. Other camps were eventually opened at Clacton, Filey, Ayr, Barry Island, Pwllheli, Bognor, Minehead, Margate, Blackpool and Brighton. His recipe was comfortable accommodation, good food, round the clock entertainment, dancing to well-known bands, indoor swimming pools, shops, bars, restaurants—all under cover. Children were particularly catered for,

with special playgrounds with all the usual fairground equipment plus aerial rides, donkeys and competitions. There were nurses on the camps to keep their eye on the children at night while mum and dad were enjoying all the entertainments. Well equipped, large theatres housed straight plays and a host of variety shows. Most of the light entertainment shows were produced by and included the famous 'Redcoats'. The Redcoats would be around all day involving themselves with the campers, running competitions and making sure they were on hand to help and advise. At night you would find the Redcoats, male and female, entertaining in the theatre and bars: singing, dancing, telling gags and working backstage.

Butlins was, and always has been, a fantastic training ground for future pros, just as the pierrots and concert party beach shows had been in the past. Redcoats were really proud to be part of the Butlin group and it wasn't easy to become a Redcoat. The performers who have reached the top from being a Butlin Redcoat are many: Dave Allen, Des O'Connor, Freddie 'Parrot Face' Davis, Roy Hudd and Charlie Drake to name just a few, and through the variety shows, a host of other top-line stars.

Pontins and Warners and other smaller groups followed suit and filled a gap in the traditional British holiday market.

*I saw two little boys paddling in the sea this morning. One said to the other: 'Ain't you got dirty feet.' And the other one said: 'Well, we never had a holiday last year.'*

## A typical seaside sketch

### BROWN EYES

*(Tabs open to reveal wife and lover embracing)*

WIFE: Oh, Mr Brown, it is good of you to come round to keep me company while my husband is out this evening.

LOVER: Darling! What time will he be home?

WIFE: Not until midnight; he's gone to a reunion dinner.

BOTH: Darling! (they embrace)

*(Tabs close)*
*(Enter husband and friend)*

FRIEND: Well old boy, jolly good night want't it?

HUSBAND: Yes, great do, pity it broke up early; still, my wife will be glad to have me home early for a change!

FRIEND: Charming wife you have too, old boy! Such lovely brown eyes!

HUSBAND: Brown eyes? Are you sure? They're blue, old bean!

FRIEND: My dear fellow, do you mean to say you don't know the colour of your wife's eyes? You husbands are all the same! They're brown my dear fellow!

*(They exit arguing)*
*Tabs open on wife and lover – still at it!*
*(Enter Husband and friend talking loudly)*
*Lover hides behind sofa.*
*Husband goes over to wife – looks into her eyes.*

HUSBAND: My god! Brown!

LOVER: Who told you I was here?

*BLACKOUT*

---

In 1897 a small band of beach and concert entertainers thought they might form themselves into a group and put aside a small sum of money when they were working to help one another through the hard times of illness or 'resting'. This they did. They called themselves The Concert Artistes Association and Benevolent Fund. It grew and grew. They now own their own freehold club premises with bar and restaurant in Bedford Street in London. Past Presidents from their membership have all worked at the seaside at some time or another. Nan Kenway (with Douglas Young), Helen Hill, Elsie and Doris Waters, Cyril Fletcher, Jack Warner, Cardew Robinson, Hugh Lloyd, Arthur Askey, Leslie Crowther, David Nixon and myself.

The people directly connected with seaside entertainment that I have talked to, agree that although it was a hard life, it was all very rewarding. The general feeling of happiness and gaiety that a 'troupe' generated amongst holiday makers and resident alike in a particular town, made it all worthwhile. The dedication that performers gave to their little shows, I think, was quite wonderful when you consider the odds they had stacked against them: bad weather; working on the sands on a platform or crude pavilion that could get blown away by the wind or washed out to sea by the tide; at the end of the day having to walk back to your digs in costume or make-up, with sometimes a pittance as your share of the 'bottle'; perhaps not being allowed by the landlady to enter her house in your make-up and therefore having to wash off on the beach in a bucket of salt-water dredged from the sea. There have been sad moments, but on reflection they now seem to be amusing to the people that were involved.

The cover of a concert party album, written by Greatrex Newman and composed by Fred Cecil. First published in 1918

# ODDS & ENDS.

## A · CONCERT · PARTY · ALBUM ·

**ODDS · WRITTEN BY** *Greatrex Newman*

**ENDS · COMPOSED BY** Fred Cecil *Reg. mark* → X

— COMPRISING —

**OPENING CHORUS ·**
(AN EXCUSE FOR BEGINNING)

**SEASIDE ALPHABET ·**
(HUMOROUS SONG, DUET,
TRIO, OR QUARTETTE)

**ITALIO DE LINGO ·**
(HUMOROUS CHARACTER
TRIO OR QUARTETTE)

**SIX LITTLE EGGS ·**
(A DOLEFUL DITTY)

**PURITANS ·**
(HUMOROUS CHARACTER
QUARTETTE)

**THE BELLE
AND THE BOBBIES ·**
(HUMOROUS MUSICAL SKETCH)

**GUTTER MERCHANTS ·**
(A CHARACTER EPISODE)

**THE DAY TRIP ·**
(A HUMOROUS ENSEMBLE)

**FINALE ·**
(A CLOSING CHORUS
IN DISGUISE)

BRANT START

-- COPYRIGHT --

When Willie Cave's pavilion was smashed to matchwood at Bournemouth in a storm, all the props and costumes went with it, including a policeman's outfit that was later washed up further down the coast. This started a police hunt to find which division had 'lost' a policeman drowned. On that occasion the artistes had been roused from their beds in the middle of the night and spent the rest wading about in the sea looking for their belongings.

There have been the exciting moments and the unexpected. When Algy More signed on with a concert party called the 'Joybells', little did he know that the tour would take in India. On the visit to India in 1929, the company were asked to do a performance for the Nizam of Hyderabad and his nine wives. A special programme was printed for the occasion in gold silk.

Another performer who made a trip overseas with a concert party was comedian Leslie Sarony—the first of many overseas tours this artiste was to make during his career. Sarony was appearing in a concert party 'Moonshine' at Bexhill-on-Sea when they were offered a trip to Buenos Aires. They accepted and did a short season there. One of the most versatile artistes ever to come out of seaside shows, Leslie Sarony began his career in a touring concert party and went on to star with Jack Hylton's Band. Sarony also starred in the original production of *Show Boat* alongside Paul Robeson, Cedric Hardwicke and Marie Burke.

Teamed with Leslie Holmes, they topped variety bills all over the country as 'The Two Leslies'.

A regular broadcaster, a prolific song writer and brilliant dancer, Leslie Sarony is still performing today at the age of eighty-one, not only as an accomplished actor, but still finding time for a number of cabaret engagements singing his own hilarious comic songs 'by public demand'.

78

*Left:* Willie Cave's pitch was smashed to pieces in a gale and the remains washed out to sea (the site was below the cliff lift to the west of Bournemouth Pier)

Not a bad date for a seaside concert party!

IN THE GRACIOUS PRESENCE OF

His Exalted Highness, Lieut-General Asaf Jah, Muzaffar-ul-Mulk Wal Mamalik Nizam-ul-Mulk Nizam-ud-Dowla Nawab Mir Sir Osman Ali Khan Bahadur, Fateh Jung, Faithful Ally of the British Government, G. C. S. I., G. B. E.,

**NIZAM OF HYDERABAD.**

## RICHARD BELL

PRESENTS

# The Joybells of 1927

=== IN ===

## "FANTASY"

→ Programme. ←

### PART I.

1. Opening Chorus      "JOYBELLS"      .. *Weeks & More*
                      The Joybells
2. Joybells come up for the first time
3. Ensemble      "THAT FASCINATING MELODY"      *More*
                      The Joybells
4. An Interlude by Arthur Ackerman with assistance
5. Miss Paddy Fowler and her Violin
                      "MOTO PERPETUO"      ...      *Carl Bohm*
6. A Series of Cameos
7. Miss Bobby Burcott is so refined
8. A Short Episode
9. Algernon More and Elsa May entertain
10. The Oldest Game in the World
    *The Singer* ...      ...      ...      Jenny Wynne
    *Love as it is* ...      Bobbie Burcott and Harrington Weeks
    *Love as it was*      Elsa May and Arthur Ackerman

### INTERVAL.

### PART II.

1. Ensemble      "THE ARCADIAN BLUES"      *More*
                      The Joybells
2. A Humorous Interlude
                      "THE STARS ADVERTISE"      *Weeks*
                      Harrington Weeks
3. Arthur Ackarman and Jenny Wynne
         with some Old English and Folk Songs
         (Collected, arranged and composed by themselves)
4. Miss Vivianne Starr in her male impression of "Wide-awake Walter"
5. A Burlesque      "ON AND OFF THE STAGE"      *Weeks*
                 Miss Bobbie Burcott and Harrington Weeks
6. Everybody may join in this

## GOD SAVE THE KING.

Produced by      ... HARRINGTON WEEKS.
Music by         ... ALGERNON MORE.
General Manager... GEO. T. BATTY.

Chirgwin's Concert Party pitch at Westcliff-on-Sea. Directly below this now is a large swimming pool

The seaside show has always produced its special characters. George Lacey, still going strong in his mid-seventies, and Alan Gale who, during a bad season at Redcar, used his company to sell ice creams on the beach during the day. From those profits he visited America and brought back some ideas which he introduced into his future concert parties.

Alan Gale also ran a short pantomime season at the Palace Theatre, Middlesbrough, near to the docks. He had a stage manager who was also playing several parts in the pantomime— you didn't have a lot of rest in a 'Gale' production!

The Pantomime was *Red Riding Hood* and on the eve of the production there was still no costume for Red Riding Hood. At the last minute Alan Gale sent his stage manager out to get some red crepe paper which he hoped could be draped round the girl to give the effect of a costume. The stage manager scoured Middlesbrough but was unable to find any red crepe paper. He came back to the theatre and reported this to Gale who, quite unruffled, said, 'Oh well, never mind, we'll do *Dick Whittington*'.

This rather proves how silly it is to get yourself worked up in our business over the 'little' things.

Advertisements in the trade paper *The Stage* could cause a certain amount of amusement and curiosity: 'Comedian wanted for concert party; must be able to cut sandwiches', and 'Young man has novelty; can be seen working'.

There were the extraordinary stories. A concert party (ENSA by then), touring England at the beginning of the 1939-45 war, was returning to its base one very dark night in a coach. It was late as the second show had been delayed and, because the artistes wanted to be out of the coach as quickly as possible on their return to billet, they were all sitting in the front of the coach. Going over a level crossing they were hit by a train and the rear half of the coach was sliced off.

80

## The Twinkle Dolls by Eric Merriman
## a sketch from 'Beyond our Ken'

KENNETH: Tonight, therefore, we pay tribute to those stalwarts of any English seaside — the Summer Concert Party. That gallant band of entertainers who every year, night after night, drive holidaymakers out into the rain again.

DOUGLAS: Ladies and gentlemen, we present:

ORCHESTRA: *FANFARE*

DOUGLAS: 'The Twinkle Dolls' or 'Keep Right on to the End of the Pier'.

ORCHESTRA: *MUSIC*

KEN W: The scene is one of our lesser known resorts — in fact, it's more of a last resort — BOGGLESHAM. A little place situated on the East Coast. Except when the tide comes in; then it's on the West Coast.

HUGH: For the past few months Bogglesham had been busily preparing to welcome the summer visitors. They'd sprayed the beach with tar, put 'No Parking' notices all along the front, and planned easy terms for the hire of transistor radios.

DOUGLAS: This, then, was Bogglesham. The time — June.

GRAMS: *CRASH OF THUNDER AND TORRENTIAL RAIN*

BILL: (NORTH COUNTRY) I told you we should never have come to this place.

BETTY: Oh, chuck it, you're always complaining.

BILL: Well, it's not much fun, is it? The cardboard on me cowboy hat's gone all soggy.

BETTY: I can't help the weather.

BILL: No, but if I'd had my way we'd have just stayed home in Manchester.

DOUGLAS: But it wasn't only the early holidaymakers who were having their problems. Down at the end of the Pier the Twinkle Dolls were re-hearsing for the start of another season.

OMNES: *MURMURS OF CONVERSATION*

HUGH: All right, boys and girls, we'll try the opening chorus once more. Olive. Olive, dear, put down the gin and get back to the piano. Right, here we go.

OMNES: (EXCEPT KENNETH) *TO PIANO ACCOMPANIMENT*
Hello to everyone,
The curtain's up and the show has begun
The Twinkle Dolls are off on a merry spree
With song and dance, a smile or two,
We've lots of good things in store for you

So if you haven't anything much else to do
We'd love the pleasure of your company.

You'll see the things we've done
To make the evening a riot of fun.
And we hope that very soon you'll all agree
The weather may be cloudy and grey,
Who cares, let's all be terribly gay,
And turn a filthy night into a sunny day
With the pleasure of your company.

(AT THE END OF SONG, THE LAST NOTE IS VERY ROPEY AND ALL GABBLE HEATEDLY)

HUGH: Boys and girls . . . please . . . please . . .

KEN W: Well, it's *her* . . . she's always going off-key.

BETTY: I am not.

KEN W: Oh yes you are. A right messy soprano.

BETTY: *Mezzo* soprano.

KEN W: Have you looked at yourself lately?

BETTY: You can talk, Meredith Frinton . . . huh . . . the debonair darling of the landladies . . .

KEN W: *I* can't help it if I'm the best juvenile lead in the country.

BILL: You're the *oldest* juvenile lead in the country.

KEN W: You keep out of this, Hedley Hanson, or I'll tear that astrakhan collar off your blazer. You should read your theatrical papers more closely. Then you'd have seen what they said about me last year . . . 'The Bobby Daren of Babbacombe'.

BILL: And what about my write up, then? . . . 'Hedley Hanson supplied all the laughs'.

KEN W: Yes . . . while you were singing Pagliacci.

BETTY: Oh, take no notice, Hedley . . . etc . . .

BILL, KEN W, ALTERCATION.

HUGH: All right, all right, that's enough. Now, it's no good us all getting upset like this. We can't expect to have everything right in the thirtieth week of rehearsal. Trouble is I detect a certain lack of togetherness among us . . . except for our soubrette and tenor, of course . . . and we all know about *their* togetherness. Anyhow, I'm sure it'll be all right on the night — or my name isn't Happy Harry Halliday, Principal comic — a laugh a minute and a gag for every occasion.

BILL: Well, shove one in your mouth now, here comes the Corporation Manager, Mr Septimus.

KENNETH: (COMING ON) Hello, everyone.

| | |
|---|---|
| HUGH: | Hello, Mr Septimus, and on behalf of all of us I'd like to say — it's quite a corporation you've got. |
| KENNETH: | Thank you. |
| HUGH: | You must be very proud of Bogglesham. |
| KENNETH: | Oh, yes, it gets more popular every year. Recently we've been having a lot of these big political conferences here, you know. |
| HUGH: | I suppose that makes quite a difference? |
| KENNETH: | Rather. For one thing, the donkeys on the beach haven't any hind legs left. |
| HUGH: | Yes, well . . . I don't think you've met everybody. This is Gwen Whittaker, our very versatile singer, who does a bit of everything. Paper tearing, glove puppets and bending iron bars. |
| KENNETH: | Yes. Well, I won't shake hands. How do you do. |
| BETTY: | Pleased to meet you. I can also throw my voice. |
| KEN W: | Yes, you should throw it away. |
| HUGH: | Oh . . . and this is Meredith Frinton. |
| KEN W: | Hello, Mr Septimus. I'm pleased to have you know me. |
| HUGH: | And now I want you to meet a beautiful and enchanting member of our Company. |
| KEN W: | But you've already introduced me. |
| HUGH: | I'm talking about Sally. Our very lovely soubrette and piano accordionist — Sally Tremaine. |
| EILEEN: | Hello, Mr Septimus. |
| HUGH: | Isn't she pretty as a picture? |
| KENNETH: | Y-e-s . . . she hasn't got a bad frame, either. |
| HUGH: | You're right, there. Lovely figure our little Sally. Mind you, she has to go carefully with her piano accordion. Anyway, lastly, I want to introduce Hedley Hanson. |
| BILL: | How do you do. |
| HUGH: | Tenor. |
| KEN W: | That's about all he's worth. |
| KENNETH: | Well, it's been a pleasure meeting you all. I'm sure this will be a very happy little show by the sea and I only wish I could be cast in it. |
| HUGH: | Don't go yet, Mr Septimus. Stay and watch the rehearsal. We're just about to hear from our tenor, Hedley Hanson. Righto, Hedley. |
| BILL: | Thank you. Olive, dear, could you give me a middle C. |

| | |
|---|---|
| ORCHESTRA: | *DENNIS TRIES SEVERAL NOTES.* |
| BILL: | Middle C, love. It's the one half way up on the right. It's marked with a pencil. *DENNIS STRIKES RIGHT NOTE.* That's it. BILL SINGS . . . 'Because' (THIS IS A TERRIBLE QUAVERING NOTE) |
| BETTY: | Oh, doesn't he sing lovely. I just love that tremor he has in his voice. |
| KEN W: | That's not a tremor, dear, he's standing on a loose floorboard. |
| HUGH: | You're right. Careful of them floorboards, Hedley. The sea comes up at high tide and the salt water's rotted 'em. |
| BILL: | All right. I'll try my encore now. CLEARS THROAT. In answer to your wonderful ovation I shall sing a grand old favourite. Thank you. *GETS NOTE FROM PIANO.* SINGS. Oh, I do like to be beside the seaside . . . |
| F/X: | *TERRIBLE SPLINTERING OF TIMBERS* |
| F/X: | *SWANEE WHISTLE DESCENDING: AND LOUD SPLASH* |
| KEN W: | Well, he's got his wish. |
| HUGH: | Eee, this is terrible. |
| BETTY: | It's tragic. What are we going to do? The show opens in a few nights. |
| KENNETH: | Well, er, I know this is going to sound ludicrous but if you're really in trouble perhaps I could help out. |
| BETTY: | Can you sing, Mr Septimus? |
| KENNETH: | Well, I'm more of a baritone than a tenor. In fact, I remember once I sang Old Man River so low I nearly drowned myself. |
| BETTY: | I think it's a marvellous idea. What do you think, Harry? |
| HUGH: | Well . . . er . . . I don't know. |
| KEN W: | It's all very well but has he any experience? |
| KENNETH: | Well, yes, I have done 'The Maid of the Mountains'. |
| BETTY: | Well, I think we should take a chance. |
| HUGH: | All right. After all, this is an emergency. Mr Septimus, welcome to the Twinkle Dolls. |
| KENNETH: | Thank you, I'm very honoured. |
| BETTY: | What's up with Meredith — he looks a bit worried. |
| KEN W: | Oh, I was just thinking about something, that's all. |
| HUGH: | All right, Meredith, out with it. What's on your mind? |

| | | | |
|---|---|---|---|
| KEN W: | Well, I . . . oh, it doesn't really matter. | KEN W: | You're a China Doll; You're a Fol-de-Rol, You're a Punch and Judy Show. |
| HUGH: | Come on, lad, if you've got something to say, say it. | EILEEN: | And when you're away from me, I'm lonely and forlorn, |
| KEN W: | Well . . . er . . . | KEN W: | I'm just like a lolly stick When all the iced lolly's gorn. |
| HUGH: | Go on. | | |
| KEN W: | I was just thinking . . . | EILEEN: | To me, you're a hat with 'Kiss Me Quick', You're a speedboat trip for two, |
| HUGH: | Yes? | | |
| KEN W: | Hadn't we better go and fish old Hedley out of the sea? | KEN W: | You're a Bingo Hall; You're a Winkle Stall, Which means that I love you. |

KEN W: Hadn't we better go and fish old Hedley out of the sea?

*ORCHESTRA: MUSIC LINK*

KEN W: We managed to reel him in with the help of the fishermen although one of them kept wanting to throw him back in. He was all right but he couldn't sing because the salt water had rusted his pipes.

So we opened with our new member, Mr Septimus. There he was, completely without experience, untrained, nervous and yet he walked out onto that stage and you should have heard him. He was diabolical!

BETTY: Still, the show went on, that's what matters. We had a packed house on opening night and they seemed to be enjoying it . . .

*ORCHESTRA: SHOW TYPE MUSIC LINK* (NOT 'SHOW BUSINESS' PLEASE)

*GRAMS: APPLAUSE*

HUGH: Thank you, thank you. And now ladies and gentlemen, here they are, Bogglesham's favourite Two in Harmony . . . Meredith Frinton and Sally Tremaine.

*ORCHESTRA: PIANO PLAY ON . . .*

*GRAMS: APPLAUSE*

KEN W: Thank you. You're very kind. Tonight Sally and I would like to sing a medley of our hit. A number which we had the pleasure of recording recently . . . on our tape recorder.

EILEEN & KEN W AND

*ORCHESTRA: INTRO AND INTO NUMBER . . .*

KEN W: Whoever could forget that holiday

EILEEN: A week-end in Sussex for two.

KEN W: Now on any seaside holiday Everything reminds me of you . . .

To me you're a stick of Candy Floss, You're a pebble on the shore,

EILEEN: You're a putting green; you're a Weight machine,

KEN W You're What the Butler Saw.

EILEEN: To me you're a plate of jellied eels, You're the donkeys in a row,

EILEEN: To me, you're the smell of that ozone,
KEN W: You're a bunch of seaweed, too, You're a Military Band; You're a bucket of sand Which means that I love . . .

EILEEN: Which means that I love . . .

TOGETHER: Which means that I love you.
(APPLAUSE)

HUGH: Lovely, lovely. And now I'm going to be joined by our baritone who at such short notice stepped right in, with lovely Gwen Whittaker and we've got a little comedy song all about the seaside. Thank you.

*ORCHESTRA: MUSIC INTRO AND INTO . . .*

HUGH, It's all going on here tonight
BETTY AND Yes, it's all going on here tonight.
KENNETH: The beaches in August are really a riot, And it isn't that easy to find piece and quiet, But I've just found the piece, now I hope she keeps quiet.
It's all going on here tonight.

It's all going on here tonight, Yes, it's all going on here tonight The Lifeguard is handsome and brave as can be, He spends all his time saving girls from the sea, Remind me to ask him to save one for me It's all going on here tonight.

It's all going on here tonight, Yes, it's all going on here tonight. The Hotel we stay at is always the same, A young couple arrived and it was such a shame, Cos, believe it or not, Smith was really their name It's all going on here tonight . . . Oh, yes . . . It's all going on here tonight.

BILL: It ought to come off!
(APPLAUSE)

Jack Tripp and the author about to 'joust' in 'Nay, Nay Plantagenet' with the Fol-de-Rols, Eastbourne, 1958

The pierrots and the concert party at the seaside had managed to entertain millions of people; they have done this purely by their own skills: no help from technical aids, and with material that was as clean as a whistle. No innuendos, no blue lines, no suggestions of people's impediments and remember all the early seaside shows had six, seven and eight changes of programme—some as many as a dozen or more. But the seaside entertainers loved their work and their audiences.

It is difficult to believe now that seaside concert party companies could be treated like film stars, but they were. I had experience of this, not personally may I add, although I did make the occasional conquest, when I was at the Gorleston Pavilion (and remember this was 1955). The principal comedian, Clifford Hensley, was playing his second season with the show (previously he had done five consecutive seasons at Minehead), and he really was feted in the town wherever he went. Jack Tripp of Fol-de-Rols fame was another comedian who built up a terrific following in the Eastbourne, Brighton and Hastings area. This was all done without the exposure of television to give them a 'name'.

Holiday makers would follow their favourites round year after year and the residents used to get excited when they knew their particular favourite was returning to entertain at the 'Pavilion'. The first morning of rehearsal in the resort would be constantly interrupted by townsfolk dropping in to welcome you back and wish you luck for the season. The opening night would be as exciting for the audience as it would be for the performers. Once all the programmes were 'on' and running, all the back-log of social engagements and invitations would be caught up with. Mrs so-and-so for tea, Mr so-and-so for lunch, before-lunch drinks with this person and that person, and nearly all your Sundays, if you were not working, would be spent at someone's house for lunch and tea and probably supper too. Once the visitor had been in to see a programme or two they would get to know where the cast went for their after-show drinks, the local hotel or particular pub, and this would be the opportunity for them to buy the cast a drink and get to know them better.

They always had their favourite comedy items or songs and would let you know them. Many visitors who had enjoyed the shows would come back, some of them travelling hundreds of miles, just for the last night. Those last nights in the town were really something. All the season's favourite items would be included in the programme. Helpers would be lined up along the aisles with armfuls of presents from well-wishers. Some residents crying because the company, by now their friends, had brought gaiety and laughter into their lives, and they only had the dark winter to look forward to in their gale-swept resort. But they had their memories, pictures of the principal comedian on their mantelpiece, the hearsay that the soprano had fallen in love with the baritone during the season and the hope that they would both be back the next season and perhaps marry in the resort. In the '20s and '30s there used to be benefit nights for certain members of the companies, special collections and presents for the particular artiste concerned.

'Summertime' at Gorlestone-on-Sea with Clifford Hensley seated behind the microphone. Marion MacLeod – now Mrs Bill Pertwee – is standing third from the left – next to that distinguished looking chap!

By 1955 television had come to stay and its impact was strengthened by the introduction of another channel in that year given over to commercial advertising. At the same time the austerity of the 1939-45 war was being forgotten and people were spending their money on cars, household appliances, holidays abroad, etc., and with the television boom in full swing, some sophistication had come into our lives; and the small sea-side show had to finish.

I have wondered if there are any comparisons to be drawn between present day entertainment and the era of the pierrot and concert party shows.

I suppose the pub entertainer could be likened to that period; he is a sort of minstrel who moves from hostelry to hostelry, trying to improve his 'pitch' as it were. Some publicans, when they do find a good entertainer who is popular with the customers, pay their 'minstrels' a good wage, after all they know that the beer nowadays, whoever the brewer, is all rather similar, so a good entertainer can make a difference to trade.

One could perhaps say that the holiday camp Redcoats or Bluecoats have a certain amount of the pierrot instinct about them, except, of course, they have a captive audience in a holiday camp. But they do have to keep that audience happy, whether they are playing bingo, watching the variety shows, entering the knobbly knees contest or organising a glamourous grandmother or bonny baby competition. The lads and lasses have to be host and personal friend to thousands of holidaymakers every year and of course act as 'Uncle' and 'Auntie' to the many thousands of children who stay at holiday camps during the summer.

Children's entertainers are still in great demand nowadays, not only for morning and afternoon performances at the seaside but for galas and fetes and children's parties in the winter and for the Christmas festivities. Many of them perform in the inland parks during the school summer holidays. These entertainers are extremely hard working, many of them doing up to two hours at a time on their own various types of

'The Pathetic History of a Seaside Performer'
1893

puppets, marionettes, magic and a variety of games involving the children which generally includes a little prize for each and every one of the children who have taken part.

Although I have great admiration for their hard work and professionalism, the difference between these children's entertainers and the pierrot is that they are paid by contract, and quite rightly so, whereas the early pierrot had to rely on 'bottling' and therefore could never be sure whether he would eat a regular meal at the end of the day.

There are various parts of London and other big cities, like Liverpool and Edinburgh, where small groups of actors are to be found at lunchtime or early evening performing, alfresco style, new one-act plays of about an hour's duration. These performances are given in courtyards or business premises and on church lawns. The old Covent Garden Market is one present venue for this sort of thing. There is no charge to the audience who come and go as they please, but a collection is sometimes taken. The actors are professional and get paid by whichever fringe group they are working for, who in turn receive a grant from the Arts Council or their City Fathers or both. This does give an opportunity for some young actors and actresses to gain experience outside repertory companies which cannot possibly absorb all of those who enter the business each year.

Perhaps then this sort of open air entertainment is the nearest thing to the alfresco entertainment our fathers and grandfathers knew. Again, however, the main difference is in the form the performers receive their payment.

Perhaps our grandparents were lucky that they did not have to suffer the coming of the television age— particularly some of the so-called 'light' entertainment.

Lord Reith was called by some people a broadcasting dictator. He was in some ways, but he liked discipline and he thought what he was doing was right, and when you think of some of the crudity that we have to put up with now, perhaps he was.

The theatre is supposed to be more sophisticated and freer in its views. I believe this freedom has helped to lower our standards, not improve them.

If Lord Reith and his establishment, and some of the earlier seaside show promoters would have been shocked and dismayed by the decline in the standard of broadcasting and the theatre over the past twenty years, what would they have said about the unadulterated filth that is purveyed in the guise of entertainment in many of the 'mixed' social and cabaret clubs throughout the country? The managements and proprietors of these establishments should have been put out of business a long time ago. They have given the whole of that particular scene a bad name, when in fact there are a few clubs that have managed to keep a standard of wholesome family entertainment.

If only 'clubland' would realise how little respect their visiting artistes have for them. Of course audiences could have put a stop to it long ago by staying away from the venues. Unfortunately, over a long period of time they have been educated to a very low standard of entertainment. Even 'mum and dad' have become resigned to accept what they are given.

Although I am sure the beach shows and concert party troupes would not have survived in their original form, I don't think we should have allowed the standard of our entertainment, in all mediums, to have suffered in the way it has, when it was given such a good start by people who really cared about the word 'entertainment'.

One very rainy afternoon at Margate
two pierrots were sitting in their pavilion
waiting for the weather to break. Outside
there were a thousand sodden, empty
deckchairs stretched out in front of
them. To pass the time they wrote the
following, for their own amusement.
Perhaps they didn't quite realise, as they
were sitting in their little summer 'house'
writing these few lines, that time was
running out for pierrot.

We're the last of Britain's pierrots, two
    optimistic heroes
We've played every beach from Blundell
    Sands to Bude,
To an audience all sitting with their
    crosswords or their knitting,
And to small boys who made noises
    which to say the least were rude.

One Bank Holiday at Sandown, the rain
    it simply ran down
But we carried on completely in a daze.
And at Weymouth our soprano, caught
    her head in the piano,
Still we got it out at Walton-on-the-
    Naze.

One Whit-Monday up at Clacton we put
    a brand new act on
We performed to two small children with
    with their dolls
Tho' they heard our opening chorus they
    hadn't much time for us
'Cos they thought they'd come to see the
    'Fol-de-Rols'.

So just spare a thought for pierrot when
    the temperature's at zero
As he sings through mists and rain in
    early May.
He really feels appalling for there's a gap
    in the tarpaulin
And the wind blows up his trousers on
    'The Road to Mandalay'.

We've been pushed into the background
    by the progress of events,
For on the beach at Brighton where we
    used to pitch our tents,
They've built a place for 'Ladies' and
    another one for 'Gents'
For pierrot isn't wanted any more.

A concert party pitch at Marine Sands,
Margate, 1910 (*Kent County Library*)

But pierrot was wanted again. In the early 1960s the writer Eric Merriman, the son of Percy Merriman who ran 'The Roosters' concert party at one time, was writing a very successful radio series 'Beyond our Ken' in which I was appearing. Eric was staying with me at Brighton and one evening we went over to see a show called 'Starlight' on the Pier at Eastbourne.

This show had been headed for many years with incredible success by Sandy Powell. (His radio catchphrase was 'Can you hear me mother?') It was a very wet and windy night when we paid them a visit. The sea was lashing up through the pier decking and during the performance the sound of the show was sometimes difficult to hear above the noise of the sea and wind. We were both impressed by the standard of this pier show and by the brilliance of Sandy Powell's comedy. His timing and comedy instinct was on a par with the greats. When we met him in the dressing room after the show, he

The cast of 'Beyond our Ken'

kept us amused for a long time with his reminiscences and recollections of seaside proprietors and performers. This all prompted Eric Merriman to write a piece for one of our radio shows. He entitled the piece 'The Twinkle Dolls'. In the audience when we recorded the show at the BBC's Paris studio in Lower Regent Street, was Sandy Powell and his wife Kay. Sandy loved the piece and it was a great success. It was later put on record and today is still one of the funniest pieces of radio to listen to. A lasting reminder perhaps of an age of entertainment we shall never see again. Seaside entertainment on the beaches and promenades started in the 1850s and lasted over a hundred years in its simple yet effective form. I wonder if in a hundred years' time people will be able to look back with the same affection on to-day's entertainment scene.

## Some of the leading Pierrot and Concert Party companies performing from the early 1900s to 1939.

Ernest Binn's 'The Arcadian Follies'
'Adeler and Sutton's Pierrot's'

Ronald Frankau's 'The Blues'
Richard Jerome's 'Brevity'
Charles Heslop's 'The Brownies'
Gane and Morley's (later Will Seymoor's) 'Bubbles'

Walter Paskin's 'Come to the Show'
Ronald Frankau's 'The Cabaret Kittens'
Ernest Crampton's 'The Cigarettes'
Charles Wade's 'The Concord Follies'
Will Ambro's 'The Criterions'
Ernest Crampton's 'The Curios'
'Catlin's Royal Pierrots'
Fred Rome's 'Costume Concert Party'

Eric Ross's 'Dazzle'

Arthur Ackerman's 'The Entertainers'
Reg Maddox's 'Evening Follies'

Murray Ashford's 'Felixstowe Entertainers'
Charlie Beanland's 'Frills and Flounces'
H. G. Pelissier's 'The Follies'

Robert Carr's 'The Georgians'
Gane and Morley's 'The Gypsies'
Wilson James's 'The Gaieties'

Harry Bright's 'Hilarity'

Donald Gilbert's 'The Ideals'
Reg Northall and Harry Turner's 'The Irresponsibles'

Gane and Morley's 'The Jack o' Lanterns'

Davey Burnaby's 'The March Hares'
Norman Langford's 'The Manx Mascots'
Harry Ruming's (later his son, Leonard Henry's) 'The Mountebanks'

Ivan Grey's 'The Ne'er-do-Wells'
Will Ambro's 'The New Superbs'
Harry East's 'The Novelty Follies'

Tom Howell's 'The Opieros'

Wilfred Lewe's 'Peepshow'
Gane and Morley's 'Pierrot, Pierrette and Piano'
Leslie Weston's 'The Playtime Follies'
Gane and Morley's 'Punchinelli'

Billy Manders' 'The Quaintesques'
Braham Fox's 'The Quixotes'

Sidney James's 'The Royal Strolling Players'
Frank Dunlop's 'The Rhapsodies'
Bart Brady's 'The Rogues'
Percy Merriman's 'The Roosters'

Richard Jerome's 'The Strolling Players'
Wolsley Charles's 'The Scamps'
Harry Leslie's 'The Seven Nobodies'
Ernest Crampton's 'So this is Romance'
Miss Shearson's 'The Society Six and their Pianist'
Albert Lyon's 'The Summit'

Lowis Rhill's 'The Tatlers'
Gane and Morley's 'The Tourists'
Fred Karno's 'Three Bites'

Carlton Fredericks' 'Les Vivandieres'

Richard Jerome's 'The Wits'

## Acknowledgements

A lot of the research for this book was carried out during a countrywide tour with the stage version of 'Dad's Army'. If I bored my fellow actors with revelations of facts and figures that to me were important, they didn't show it and still talk to me.

During a pantomime season in London, I shared a dressing room with heavyweight actor Roy Kinnear, and spent a considerable amount of time going through more than twenty double-sided tape recordings taken from conversations with contributors to this book. When Roy sees me now he runs, or rolls, away from me as fast as possible.

On quite a few visits to places and people, I was accompanied by that charming and talented actor, the late Edward Sinclair, and although he never showed it, I am sure he must have wished at times that he had been somewhere else other than with me.

I have a special thanks to make to the man who opened it all up for me: Algernon (Algy) More. He has been a sincere and amusing friend for nearly twenty years. His associations with summer entertainment go back many years, in fact to his radio and music hall career with a wonderful comedy and musical act, Vine More and Nevard. When I told Algy that I proposed to write a book on the history of seaside entertainment, he gave me a lot of his time, for which I am truly grateful.

Joe Ging, the curator of the Sunderland Theatre Museum, and his wife Heather, have been an enormous help and their enthusiasm has been a constant inspiration. (Incidentally, this museum is now closed, but Joe Ging has re-housed the collection in Newcastle.)

Gwen Adeler was most generous in spending time to talk to me about her father Edwin, and although in her eighties, her memory was remarkable.

Geoffrey Mellor, the Bradford Seaside Historian, was most kind and I treasure his little book *Pom-poms and Ruffles* which deals with the northern pierrot scene.

George Fairweather, at Bournemouth, never seemed to mind when, on several occasions, I interrupted him in his hairdressing salon to prise further information out of him.

Powis Pinder and his wife made me most welcome in their Isle of Wight home and their anecdotes of father, Arthur Pinder's Island ventures, together with a collection of items for reproduction, is much appreciated.

Greatrex Newman was able to reveal many intimate details of the rise of the great 'Fol-de-Rols'.

Ted Goate of Yarmouth took an enormous amount of trouble in giving me details of names and dates of some fifty years of east coast entertainment. His photos have also been invaluable.

My sincere thanks to Emilie Benfield for her photos and information about the early '20s and '30s.

Chris Wortman, who became one of our premier dame comedians in pantomime, was very helpful.

Bunty Gordon, whose father, Harry, ran the Beach Pavilion, Aberdeen, was able to fill in the gaps for me about the Scottish seaside scene.

Leslie Sarony gave me an insight into the early days of touring Concert Party and this great little comedian and songwriter of 'The Two Leslies' fame is, I am glad to say, still giving audiences the benefit of his enormous talent.

Bill Ellis of Rhyl gave me all the information on the great female impersonator, Billy Manders.

Jack Storey, one of Blackpool's favourite entertainers, was very helpful, as was Max Tyler of Havant. So too was publisher and composer Gerald Benson who told me about his early connections with the seaside.

Mr Barry Pimlott gave me some lovely photos of Cleveleys entertainment and Jack Grapho companies.

Miss B. V. French loaned me some of the illustrations of Brighton.

Mona Allen supplied the pictures and information of her mother and father's troupe 'The Manx Mascots'.

My thanks to Eric Merriman, who wrote the radio piece 'The Twinkle Dolls', which is reproduced in the book and is a reminder of seaside concert party.

Southport (Miss Tarbuck), Margate (Miss Wyatt), Broadstairs, Newcastle, Bournemouth, Torquay, Weymouth, Bridlington and Blackpool public libraries have been most helpful, as have *The Yorkshire Post, Brighton Argus, Yarmouth Mercury* and BBC Radio Brighton.

My wife Marion was such a help in researching the early social back-ground —my family has lived with the preparation of this little piece for nearly three years.

# Index

Aberdeen, 37, 73
Adeler, Edwin, 15, 17-19, 21, 29
Adeler, Gwen, 19
Allandale, Fred (Bobby), 19, 36, 48
Allen, Dave, 75
Andrews, Julie, 56
Angers, Avril, 38
Arthur, Wallis, 56
Askey, Arthur, 38, 43, 45, 52, 76

Baron, Bunny, 57
Benfield, Emilie, 66, 67, 69
Benson, Gerald, 46
Binns, Ernest, 41, 48
Bishop, Neville, 63
Blackpool, 6, 7, 8, 19, 34, 35, 36, 48, 75
Bliss, Mrs Leo, 69
Bognor Regis, 56, 75
Booth, Webster, 52
Boscombe, 29, 47
Boulter, John, 43
Bournemouth, 26, 33, 35, 45, 46, 78
Brady, Bart, 41
Braham-Fox, Tom, 22, 26
Brighton, 6-8, 16, 22, 26, 36, 40-2, 75, 85
Brownbill, Bert, 66
Burke, Billy, 19
Burke, Marie, 78
Burnaby, David, 37, 71
Butlin, Sir Billy, 75

Carr, Pearl, 57
Catlin, Gladys, 26
Catlin, Will, 10, 20, 21-3, 26, 62
Cave, Willie, 45, 46, 78
Cecil, Fred, 76
Charles, Hugh, 38
Charles, Wolsley, 37, 71
Chirgwin, G.H., 10, 11
Christie, Allen, 38
Clayton, Herbert, 35
Clement, Fred, 57
Cliff, Laddie, 37
Clive, Connie, 33
Compton, Fay, 71
Cotton, Frank, 20
Courtnidge, Ciceley, 71
Cowes, 12
Crampton, Ernest, 71
Crick, Monte, 66
Crippen, Dr and Mrs Harvey, 19
Crowther, Leslie, 38, 76
Cunliffe, Whit, 19

Daly, Mark, 35
Davies, Windsor, 57
Davis, Freddie, 75
Desmond, Jack and Jerry, 61
Dixon, Reg, 38
Dodds, Billy, 71
Donald, Peter, 37
Drake, Charlie, 75
Dunn, Bobby, 28, 33

Dunn, Clive, 17, 28, 33, 43, 56

Eastbourne, 37, 58, 85
Edward VII, 8, 12, 14, 26, 33
Edwards, Maude E., 73
Elliott, G.H., 11, 29
Ellis, Bill, 26
Emery, Dick, 56
Emney, Fred, 48
Essex, Clifford, 12, 14
Estelle, Don, 57

Fairweather, George, 45, 46
Felgate, Peter, 38
Field, Sid, 61
Fletcher, Cyril, 38, 43, 76
Forsyth, Bruce, 58
Francis, Dai, 57
Francis, Day and Hunter, 8
Frankau, Ronald, 15, 66, 67, 69
Frazer, Bill, 38, 43
Fuller, Leslie, 43, 45

Gale, Alan, 80
Gideon, Melville, 37
Godfrey, Sir Dan, 45
Gordon, Harry, 73
Gorleston-on-Sea, 59, 65, 68
Gray, Clifford, 56
Gray, Eddie, 45
Gunn, Martha, 14

Hancock, Tony, 7, 45
Handley, Tommy, 19, 66
Hanson, John, 57
Hardwicke, Sir Cedric, 78
Hare, Doris, 38
Hastings, 36-7, 85
Hayes, Melvyn, 57
Henry, Leonard, 43
Hensley, Clifford, 85
Henson, Leslie and Nicky, 71
Hill, Benny, 43
Hill, Helen, 76
Holloway, Stanley, 14, 37
Holmes, Leslie, 78
Horne, Kenneth, 69, 91
Howell, Tom, 37
Howes, Bobby and Sally Anne, 43
Hudd, Roy, 75
Hulbert, Claude and Jack, 71
Hunter, Jim, 36, 42
Hylton, Jack, 38, 42, 78

Jaffa, Max, 21
Johnson, Teddy, 57
Jones, Allan and Jack, 48

Kelly, Tom, 17
Kenway and Young, 66, 76
Korris, Harry, 48

Lacy, George, 39, 80
Langford, Norman, 72
Lauder, Harry, 50

Laughton, Charles, 26
Lavender, Ian, 57
Lee, Bernard, 52
Le Mesurier, John, 7
Lever, Reg, 39
Llandudno, 19, 22, 43
Lloyd, Hugh, 43, 76
Lloyd, Marie, 19
Loraine, Violet, 56
Lynne, Frank, 17

MacDonald, Aimi, 57
MacDonald, Jeannette, 48
Mack, Uncle, 11, 13
MacLeod, Marion, 85
Maddox, Frank, 62
Maddox, Reg, 62, 63, 65
Manders, Billie, 26
Margate, 9, 43, 44, 75, 90
Merredew, Gladys, 52
Merriman, Eric, 92
Midgley, Walter, 38
Miller, Max, 40, 41
Monkman, Phyllis, 37
More, Algy, 27, 28, 78
More, Reuban, 28, 29, 32, 47
Moss, Ernie, 48
Mudd, Moses, 29
Murdoch, Richard, 38, 69

Newman, Greatrex, 34, 36, 37, 38, 76
Nixon, David, 38, 76

Oberon, Merle, 19
O'Connor, Des, 75

Paskin, Walter, 61
Pepper, Harry S., 14
Pepper, Will C., 14, 59
Phillips, F., 7
Pinder, Arthur and Powis, 51-3
Popplewell, Ben, 71, 73
Potter, Gillie, 33
Powell, Kay and Sandy, 92
Priestley, J.B., 71
Preston, Sir Harry, 42
Prince, Arthur, 29

Radford, Basil, 66
Raines, Claude and Fred, 18
Reid, Beryl, 33
Reith, Lord, 89
Robeson, Paul, 48, 78
Robey, George, 56
Robinson, Cardew, 76
Rogers, Ann, 43
Roper, Fred, 41
Ross, Eric, 21, 56
Royle, George, 34, 35, 36, 38

Rutherford, Robert, 59, 65
Ryde, 28, 29, 33, 50-1

Sanders, Chip, 58
Sarony, Leslie, 78
Scarborough, 4, 21-2, 26, 34, 35, 36, 37, 71
Scott, Terry, 43
Secombe, Harry, 43
Shadwell, Charles, 59
Shanklin, 51-2
Sheppard, Jack, 40
Skegness, 57, 75
Southend, 7, 20, 58
Southport, 8, 9, 14, 17, 18, 19, 29
Southsea, 28, 29, 32
Stanhope, Ethel, 19
Stewart, Jo, 43
Stratton, Eugene, 11
Styles, Edwin, 52
Summers, Dorothy, 19
Sutton, W.G., 17-18, 29

Tate, Wylie, 17, 19, 48
Thomas, Terry, 45, 69
Tich, Little, 11
Trevor, Enid, 71
Trinder, Tommy, 42, 57
Tripp, Jack, 38, 85

Upsom, Jack, 60

Varney, Reg, 43
Vaughan, Norman, 43
Ventnor, 28, 33, 51, 52

Waldman, Ronnie, 14
Waller, Jack, 35
Walmsley, Fred, 36, 48
Warne, F.G., 14
Warner, Jack, 38, 59, 76
Waters, Elsie and Doris, 38, 39, 59, 60, 76
Wayne, Naunton, 15, 66
West, Kathleen, 38
Western Brothers, 38
Weymouth, 14, 15, 17
White, Fred, 56
Whitley Bay, 20, 69, 71
Wilcock, Bob, 59, 65
Williams, Bransby, 19
Wilson, Fred, 45
Winters, Joan, 59
Wortman, Chris, 62, 63, 65
Wylie, Julian, 17, 19

Yarmouth, 26, 61-2, 64-5
Yule, Fred, 52

Ziegfeld, Florenz, 19